G000122926

SOCIAL INFLUENCES ON ADOLESCENT AND YOUNG ADULT ALCOHOL USE

SOCIAL ISSUES, JUSTICE AND STATUS

Additional books in this series can be found on Nova's website
under the Series tab.

Additional E-books in this series can be found on Nova's website
under the E-book tab.

SOCIAL ISSUES, JUSTICE AND STATUS

SOCIAL INFLUENCES ON ADOLESCENT AND YOUNG ADULT ALCOHOL USE

MELISSA A. LEWIS
CLAYTON NEIGHBORS
KRISTEN P. LINDGREN
KAITLIN G. BUCKINGHAM
AND
MELISSA HOANG

Novinka
Nova Science Publishers, Inc.
New York

Copyright © 2010 by Nova Science Publishers, Inc.

All rights reserved. No part of this book may be reproduced, stored in a retrieval system or transmitted in any form or by any means: electronic, electrostatic, magnetic, tape, mechanical photocopying, recording or otherwise without the written permission of the Publisher.

For permission to use material from this book please contact us:
Telephone 631-231-7269; Fax 631-231-8175
Web Site: http://www.novapublishers.com

NOTICE TO THE READER

The Publisher has taken reasonable care in the preparation of this book, but makes no expressed or implied warranty of any kind and assumes no responsibility for any errors or omissions. No liability is assumed for incidental or consequential damages in connection with or arising out of information contained in this book. The Publisher shall not be liable for any special, consequential, or exemplary damages resulting, in whole or in part, from the readers' use of, or reliance upon, this material.

Independent verification should be sought for any data, advice or recommendations contained in this book. In addition, no responsibility is assumed by the publisher for any injury and/or damage to persons or property arising from any methods, products, instructions, ideas or otherwise contained in this publication.

This publication is designed to provide accurate and authoritative information with regard to the subject matter covered herein. It is sold with the clear understanding that the Publisher is not engaged in rendering legal or any other professional services. If legal or any other expert assistance is required, the services of a competent person should be sought. FROM A DECLARATION OF PARTICIPANTS JOINTLY ADOPTED BY A COMMITTEE OF THE AMERICAN BAR ASSOCIATION AND A COMMITTEE OF PUBLISHERS.

LIBRARY OF CONGRESS CATALOGING-IN-PUBLICATION DATA

Social influences on adolescent and young adult alcohol use / Melissa A. Lewis ... [et al.].
 p. cm.
 Includes index.
 ISBN 978-1-61728-032-0 (softcover)
 1. Young adults--Alcohol use. 2. Teenagers--Alcohol use. 3. Social influence. I. Lewis, Melissa A.
 HV5135.S65 2009
 362.29'110835--dc22
                          2010016736

Published by Nova Science Publishers, Inc. † New York

CONTENTS

Preface   **vii**

Chapter 1   Introduction and Overview   **1**

Chapter 2   Social Learning Theory
                 and Social Cognitive Theory   **5**

Chapter 3   Alcohol Expectancy Theory   **11**

Chapter 4   Problem Behavior Theory   **15**

Chapter 5   Social Comparison Theory   **21**

Chapter 6   Social Identity Theory   **25**

Chapter 7   Self-Derogation Theory   **29**

Chapter 8   Theory of Reasoned Action and
                 Theory of Planned Behavior   **33**

Chapter 9   Prototype/Willingness Model   **37**

Chapter 10   Deviance Regulation Theory   **41**

Chapter 11   Peer Cluster Theory   **45**

Chapter 12   Reactance Theory   **49**

Chapter 13   Conclusion   **53**

Author Note   **55**

References   **57**

Index   **75**

PREFACE

An extensive literature has demonstrated that many adolescents and young adults engage in drinking behavior, resulting in acute and chronic negative consequences (e.g., unintentional injuries, arguments, unplanned and/or unprotected sexual activities, trouble with police/authorities, poor academic/work performance, suicide, and death), and alcohol dependence. Social influence is foremost among the causes attributed to the initiation and maintenance of alcohol use during this period. This book reviews a number of prominent theories of social influence that are directly relevant to drinking behavior among adolescents and young adults. For each theory, a brief description is provided, followed by relevant research related to adolescent and young adult drinking. Theoretical implications for preventative interventions are also discussed. Highlighted theories include: social learning theory, social cognitive theory, alcohol expectancy theory, problem behavior theory, social comparison theory, social identity theory, self-derogation theory, the theory of reasoned action, the theory of planned behavior, prototype willingness model, deviance regulation theory, peer cluster theory, and reactance theory.

Chapter 1

INTRODUCTION AND OVERVIEW

Alcohol continues to be the most widely used substance by American youth. Results from the 2008 Monitoring the Future survey found that the proportions of 8th, 10th, and 12th graders who reported drinking an alcoholic beverage in the 30-day period prior to the survey were 16%, 29%, and 43%, respectively (Johnston, O'Malley, Bachman, and Schulenberg, 2009). Moreover, research has shown that adolescence is the most common time for the initiation of alcohol use, with 39% of 8th graders having initiated alcohol use and 58% of 10th graders having initiated alcohol use. By the time high school students graduate, over 70% will have initiated alcohol use (Johnston et al., 2009). Alcohol use among adolescents is a concern, because it is a contributor to the top causes of death for youth: unintentional injuries, homicides, and suicides (Heron, 2007). Moreover, preventing or delaying the initiation of alcohol use of adolescents is of importance as research has shown that earlier initiation is related to problems in brain development and neurocognitive disadvantages, such as reduced hippocampal volumes and poorer performance on memory and spatial tasks (Brown and Tapert, 2004; Squeglia, Jacobus, and Tapert, 2009). Alcohol use in adolescence is also associated with an increased risk of developing alcohol dependence (Buchmann et al., 2009; Grant et al., 2006; Grant and Dawson, 1997; Hingson, Heeren, and Winter, 2006). For example, Buchmann and colleagues (2009) found that the age of first drink significantly predicted high-risk drinking in young adults (number of standard drinks, frequency of drinking occasions, frequency of heavy drinking occasions, and AUDIT scores). In addition, Grant and Dawson (1997) found that youth who initiated alcohol use prior to age 14, had a 41% chance of developing alcohol dependence during their lifetime compared to individuals who waited until the age of 21 to initiate alcohol use, whose chances were reduced to 10%.

Alcohol use and associated risks are also prevalent among young adults (Bingham, Shope, and Tang, 2005; Courtney and Polich, 2009; Hingson, Heeren, Winter, and Wechsler, 2005; Hingson, Heeren, Zakocs, Kopstein, and Wechsler, 2002; O'Malley and Johnston, 2002; Schulenberg and Maggs, 2002; Slutske, 2005; Substance Abuse and Mental Health Services Administration [SAMHSA], 2008; White et al., 2006). Furthermore, college students between the ages of 18 to 22 are more likely than their non-college peers to have used alcohol in the past month and to have engaged in heavy-episodic drinking. Although individuals who drink heavily in high school are less likely to attend college, alcohol use among college students increases more rapidly and eventually surpasses that of non-college peers (Bachman, Wadsworth, O'Malley, Johnston, and Schulenberg, 1997). For example, past month alcohol use was reported by 63.7% of college students in comparison to 53.5% of non-college individuals (SAMHSA, 2008). Moreover, 43.6% of college students report heavy-episodic drinking (defined as five or more drinks in a row during the previous two weeks) compared to 38.4% of their non-college peers (SAMHSA, 2008). Research continues to demonstrate that not only are young adults engaging in heavy drinking but also that they are experiencing considerable alcohol-related negative consequences including poor class/work attendance, property damage, hangovers, trouble with authorities, injuries, unprotected sex, sexual assault, and death (Abbey, Zawacki, Buck, Clinton, and McAuslan, 2004; Hingson et al., 2005; Wechsler, Davenport, Dowdall, Moeykens, and Castillo, 1994).

Because of the high prevalence rates of alcohol use and the number of negative consequences associated with alcohol use, drinking among adolescents and young adults presents an enormous public health concern. In 2007, the Acting Surgeon General of the United States issued a *Call to Action To Prevent and Reduce Underage Drinking* (U.S. Department of Health and Human Services, 2007). In addition, the National Institute on Alcohol Abuse and Alcoholism has an underage drinking research initiative that aims to intensify research, evaluation, and outreach efforts regarding underage drinking. A key to preventing alcohol use and related negative consequences in adolescents and young adults is gaining a better understanding of why individuals initiate and continue to engage in those behaviors.

Prior research has demonstrated that social influence is foremost among the causes attributed to the initiation and maintenance of alcohol use during adolescence and young adulthood (Baer, 2002; Baer, MacClean, and Marlatt,

1998; Borsari and Carey, 2001; Hawkins, Catalano, and Miller, 1992). Social influence factors include parents, family, peers, society and culture. This book reviews a number of prominent theories of social influence that are relevant to drinking behavior among adolescents and young adults. For each theory, a brief description is provided, followed by selected research related to adolescent and young adult drinking. Theoretical implications for preventative interventions are also discussed. Highlighted theories include: social learning theory, social cognitive theory, alcohol expectancy theory, problem behavior theory, social comparison theory, social identity theory, self-derogation theory, the theory of reasoned action, the theory of planned behavior, prototype/willingness model, deviance regulation theory, peer cluster theory, and reactance theory.

Chapter 2

SOCIAL LEARNING THEORY
AND SOCIAL COGNITIVE THEORY

Social learning theory applies to several theories of human behavior proposed by various prominent psychologists. These principles of learning are integrated with cognitive psychology in order to explain how social and personal factors relate to the environment. One of the most influential contributors of social learning theory is Albert Bandura (Bandura, 1969, 1977, 1986). According to social learning theory (Bandura, 1969, 1977) and later extended to social cognitive theory (Bandura, 1986), people's acquisition and maintenance of behaviors, including but not limited to health and risk behaviors, are dependent upon the interrelationships among behavior, environmental factors, and personal factors (cognitive, affective, and biological events). Social learning/cognitive theory is comprised of four major constructs: differential reinforcement, vicarious learning, cognitive processes and reciprocal determinism. Each of these principles or constructs may be applied to enhance our understanding of alcohol use among adolescents and young adults.

Differential reinforcement occurs when consequences are applied for a behavior dependent on stimulus conditions or environmental setting. Differential reinforcement is used to help explain why people's behavior often changes in different environmental settings. Positive and negative reinforcement as well as punishment are often received from the environment or from the self depending on environmental setting. For example, if an adolescent drinks alcohol at a party with friends, he may experience feelings of relaxation, participate in and enjoy social exchanges with peers, and receive social approval. However, if an adolescent drinks alcohol at home with parents, he may still experience relaxation but will likely receive disapproval and possible consequences from his parents. Whether or not an adolescent or young adult will abstain or initiate alcohol use, or continue or stop alcohol use, is dependent on past, present and future anticipated rewards and punishments attached to abstinence and alcohol use. The more an adolescent or young adult perceives alcohol use as positive and the *less* he/she experiences negative consequences for alcohol use and holds attitudes that are disapproving of alcohol use, the more likely he/she is to engage in alcohol use.

VICARIOUS LEARNING (MODELING)

Bandura also proposed that the acquisition of behavior can occur through observation of others or by communication with others. In other words, not only will direct reinforcement increase the likelihood of engaging in that behavior, but vicarious learning (e.g., seeing someone else reinforced), or modeling, of a behavior will also increase the likelihood of behavior. When applied to adolescent and young adult drinking behavior, one's drinking behavior can be affected by observing others' drinking behavior or attitudes, as well as by observing the outcomes of others' drinking behavior. Social learning/cognitive theory posits that adolescents and young adults acquire their behaviors and beliefs about alcohol from their role models, especially close friends and parents. Thus, drinking behaviors, alcohol-related expectancies and evaluations, drinking self-efficacy, and drinking refusal self-efficacy can all be acquired from the observation and modeling of role models who use and who do not use alcohol.

Experimental research has demonstrated that modeling can be predictive of alcohol consumption among adolescents and young adults. In a meta-analytic review of the literature, Quigley and Collins (1999) found that modeling had a significant effect on alcohol consumption, blood alcohol concentration, and volume per sip, such that participants increased their alcohol consumption when exposed to a heavy-drinking model in comparison to a no-model control condition and a light-drinking model. More recently, Larsen and colleagues (2009) examined the role of modeling in relation to alcohol consumption among college students in the Netherlands. Students were exposed to either a control, light-drinking, or heavy-drinking same-sex model. Unlike previous research in which participants were obligated to consume alcohol (Quigley and Collins, 1999), a design was used such that students were allowed to drink alcohol but were also allowed to choose non-alcohol beverages. Findings indicated that participants consumed significantly greater amounts of alcohol when exposed to heavy-drinking models in comparison to non-drinking and light-drinking models. Additionally, Engels and colleagues (2009) examined whether portrayal of alcohol images in movies and commercials on television promotes alcohol consumption. Male students in the Netherlands were assigned to watch a movie clip with two commercial breaks and were allowed to drink non-alcohol or alcoholic beverages. Participants were randomly assigned to one of four conditions that varied by movie (few vs. many alcohol portrayals) and commercials (alcohol not present vs. alcohol present). Participants in the many alcohol portrayals and alcohol present commercials consumed an average of 1.5 more glasses of alcohol than those in the control condition with no alcohol portrayals. Together, these experimental studies provide evidence of a causal relationship between modeling and alcohol consumption.

When examining the influence of role models, non-experimental research supports that adolescents and young adults may learn to use substances by modeling drinking behavior of parents, siblings, and peers (Andrews, Hops, and Duncan, 1997; Borsari and Carey, 2001; Casswell, Pledger, and Pratap, 2002; Duncan, Duncan, and Strycker, 2006; Latendresse et al., 2008). For example, a longitudinal study conducted by Casswell and colleagues (2002) found that parental drinking at the age of nine was found to predict offspring drinking trajectories. Additionally, a longitudinal study of young adults demonstrated that peer use of alcohol predicted binge drinking and problem use by young adults, providing evidence for a causal role of peer influence on drinking behaviors (Andrews, Tildesley, Hops, and Li, 2002).

According to social learning/cognitive theory, cognitive processes are posited to mediate environmental events and behavior. These processes include encoding, organizing, and retrieving information, all of which are postulated ultimately to regulate behavior. Thus from this viewpoint, the environment provides an individual with information that is then cognitively processed, and that, in turn, determines an individual's behavioral response. Once an individual has acquired a behavior, self-regulation and self-efficacy play a role in future engagement of that behavior. Self-regulation is the capability of arranging environment incentives and producing consequences for one's behavior. Self-efficacy is an individual's beliefs regarding the likelihood that he or she can engage in a behavior in order to produce a desired outcome.

In relation to drinking behavior, self-efficacy is often defined as confidence in one's abilities to drink or to not drink in a given situation, or across situations. According to social learning/cognitive theory, role models can shape both drinking self-efficacy and drinking refusal self-efficacy. For example, observing a peer refusing to use alcohol can enhance one's drinking refusal self-efficacy: the peer models the skills necessary to avoid using alcohol. Drinking refusal self-efficacy has been found to relate to alcohol consumption when examined in adolescent and young adult samples. For example, Epstein, Zhou, Bang, and Botvin (2007) found that adolescents who had greater decision-making skills, drinking refusal skill techniques, and skills related to resisting media influences were less likely to engage in future drinking. Young and colleagues (2006, 2007) found that drinking refusal self-efficacy specific to social pressure (e.g., when someone offers you a drink), emotional relief (e.g., when you are feeling upset), and opportunistic drinking (e.g., when you are by yourself) were negatively associated with alcohol consumption in adolescents and college students.

RECIPROCAL DETERMINISM

Bandura (1969) used the term "reciprocal determinism" to describe the interactive relationships among behavior, environmental factors, and personal factors. Briefly, reciprocal determinism suggests that change in one factor is shaped by the other two factors and vice versa. For example, change in drinking behavior is shaped by environmental and personal factors and vice versa. One's drinking behavior can also affect one's environment and peer groups, such that those who drink may select social environments in which drinking occurs or have close friends who also drink. These social environments and peers will then affect subsequent drinking behavior.

Many studies have supported the concept of reciprocal determinism among samples of adolescents and young adults. Curran, Stice, and Chassin (1997) examined reciprocal determinism in peer influences and alcohol use in an adolescent sample. Findings supported both peer socialization and peer selection: early levels of peer alcohol use were associated with later adolescent alcohol use and earlier adolescent alcohol use was associated with later levels of peer alcohol use. Research has also evaluated reciprocal determinism in personal factors, such as alcohol expectancies (see Alcohol Expectancy Theory), and alcohol use among adolescents (Mitchell, Beals, and Kaufman, 2006; Sher, Wood, Wood, and Raskin, 1996; Smith, Goldman, Greenbaum, and Christiansen, 1995). For example, Mitchell and colleagues (2006) found that in a sample of Native American adolescents and young adults, alcohol use and outcome expectancies were interrelated, providing support for reciprocal determinism between these two constructs.

Read, Wood, and Capone (2005) examined reciprocal determinism in social influence, alcohol use and related negative consequences among young adults transitioning to college. Findings indicated a reciprocal relationship between active and passive social influence and alcohol use. Specifically, pre-matriculation alcohol use offers and social modeling predicted sophomore year alcohol use, and pre-matriculation alcohol use predicted sophomore year alcohol use offers and social modeling. However, when examining alcohol-related negative consequences, environmental selection was supported rather than reciprocal determinism. Specifically, alcohol-related negative consequences at pre-matriculation predicted alcohol use offers and social modeling during sophomore year, but only social modeling at pre-matriculation was marginally associated with alcohol-related negative consequences during sophomore year. Thus, this study provided support for reciprocal determinism for alcohol use, but not alcohol-related negative consequences. Additional research is needed to further evaluate reciprocal determinism in consequences associated with drinking among adolescents and young adults.

SUMMARY AND IMPLICATIONS

Social learning/cognitive theory suggests that the acquisition and maintenance of health and risk behaviors results from the interrelationships among behavior, environmental factors, and personal factors. Primary constructs of this theory have received support from alcohol literature pertaining to adolescents and young adults, which suggests that interventions that address the impact of social influence on drinking by including drinking refusal skills training and drinking moderation strategies may be beneficial (Larimer et al., 2007; Schinke, Cole, and Fang, 2009). For example, recent research found that drinking moderation strategies mediated the efficacy of a mailed alcohol feedback intervention (Larimer et al., 2007) in a sample of college students. Participants who received the intervention were more likely to use protective behavior strategies (such as limiting the number of alcoholic drinks consumed or using a designated driver) more frequently and the use of protective behavior strategies was associated with subsequent reductions in alcohol use. In addition, social learning/cognitive theory suggests that prevention efforts should try to make role models who approve of or use alcohol less salient and role models who disapprove of or do not use alcohol more salient.

Chapter 3

ALCOHOL EXPECTANCY THEORY

Alcohol expectancy theory originates from basic psychological theories and was extended to the domain of alcohol. More technically known as alcohol expectancy *outcome* theory (see Goldman, Del Boca, and Darkes, 1999; Jones, Corbin, and Fromme, 2001), the theory is derived from general expectancy outcome theory, which incorporates both basic principles of learning as well as cognitive constructs (e.g., Bandura, 1977; MacCorquodale and Meehl, 1953; Rotter, 1954; Tolman, 1932). Briefly, expectancy outcome theories propose that behavior is governed not only by reinforcement and punishment (basic learning theory), but also by one's expectations of the future (positive or negative) reinforcement outcomes associated with engaging in that behavior. It is argued that the reinforcement outcomes associated with a behavior can be learned and are stored in memory and that one's expectations of those outcomes influence future behavior. Consistent with social learning models (e.g., Bandura, 1969, 1977, 1986), these expectancies can be learned through direct and indirect experience. There is ongoing debate regarding the extent to which these expectancies are consciously versus non-consciously held and/or whether their influence on behavior is "automatic" or "spontaneous," but theory proponents appear to agree that expectancies have, at a minimum, a significant automatic or non-conscious component (see Goldman et al., 1999; Thush and Wiers, 2007).

Regarding applications of expectancy outcome theories to alcohol, specifically; the behavior (alcohol consumption) is predicted to occur as a function of one's expectations of reinforcement outcomes. Alcohol outcome expectancies (AOE) are predicted to *vary across* persons as a function of their learning histories – i.e., to the extent that individuals have similar/different drinking experiences, they will have similar/different AOEs. They are also predicted to vary *within persons* as a function of their learning histories --i.e., to the extent that a person has different experiences with or makes changes to their drinking over time, that person's AOEs will change. Finally, although at first glance, AOE theory may seem an unlikely representative of social influence theories *per se*, it is important to note that some of the effects of alcohol are psychological (versus pharmacological) and that AOEs appear to be learned from peers, parents, mass media as well as from direct experience with alcohol (see Abrams and Niaura, 1987; MacAndrew and Edgerton, 1969; Maisto, Carey, and Bradizza, 1999). Accordingly, it can be stated that AOEs are, at least partially, a product of and/or subject to social influence.

Consistent with theories of AOE, people can develop AOEs well before they begin to drink. For example, AOEs have been measured in children as young as eight years of age, and research suggests that there are critical periods – in particular, late childhood and early adolescence – for the development of AOEs (Dunn and Goldman, 1998; Miller, Smith, and Goldman, 1990). It also appears that as children's AOEs shift as they age and mature into drinking– e.g., they seem to change from having largely negative AOEs to more positive AOEs (Miller et al., 1990; Schell, Martino, Ellickson, Collins, and McCaffrey, 2005). As suggested by AOE theories, children's and adolescents' AOEs (a) are correlated with alcohol use, exposure to alcohol advertisements, and peer and parental use and approval of use (see Martino, Collins, Ellickson, Schell, and McCaffrey, 2006); and (b) predict incremental variance in drinking behavior, particularly with respect to the quantity (vs. frequency) of drinking (see Jones et al., 2001). Moreover, adolescents' pre-drinking AOEs have been found to predict changes in drinking in prospective studies (Goldman et al., 1999; Jones et al., 2001). Finally, advanced statistical methods enabled the testing of models that specify reciprocal prospective relations between adolescents' AOEs and their drinking behaviors. Consistent with AOE theory, there is evidence of a reciprocal relationship between alcohol use and AOE, providing support for the claim that changes in expectancies predict changes in drinking and vice-versa (e.g., Mitchell et al., 2006; Sher et al., 1996; Smith et al., 1995).

Research on young adults, which largely focuses on college students, also indicates that AOEs are associated with alcohol consumption, including problematic drinking (see Baer, 2002; Ham and Hope, 2003; Jones et al., 2001). It appears that positive AOEs are most commonly and consistently linked to alcohol consumption (Baer, 2002; Ham and Hope, 2003; but see also Jones et al., 2001), and that AOEs predict future drinking behavior over time

(Blume, Schmaling, and Marlatt, 2003; Carey, 1995; Kidorf et al., 1995, cf. Ham and Hope, 2003). Other studies have found that negative AOEs also are positively correlated with college students' alcohol consumption and that they predict incremental variance in drinking above and beyond positive AOEs (e.g., Jones et al., 2001, Valdiva and Stewart, 2005). Related to these findings is a debate within the alcohol field about (a) which AOEs are "truly" negative from the point of view of those being studied and (b) whether measurement of AOEs should also include assessments of a person's evaluation of the AOE (i.e., is the AOE positive or negative?) (e.g., Fromme, Stroot, and Kaplan, 1993). Consistent with these issues, Neighbors and colleagues (2007) found that negative AOEs, in comparison to positive AOEs, are uniquely and positively predictive of alcohol-related problems. Neighbors et al. also found that viewing negative AOE more positively was associated with more alcohol-related problems. Beyond AOE valence and measurement concerns, recent research has also turned to identifying moderators of AOE, including gender (Jones et al., 2001), anxiety sensitivity (O'Connor, Farrow, and Colder, 2008), self-efficacy (Gilles, Turk, and Fresco, 2006), and sexual orientation (Hatzenbuehler, Corbin, and Fromme, 2008) and examining AOE as a mediator (e.g., Goldman et al., 1999; Hatzenbuehler, et al., 2008; McCarthy, Aarons, and Brown, 2002).

Summary and Implications

AOEs seem to be consistent predictors of adolescent and young adult drinking. However, many important questions remain. First and foremost, there is a debate in the field about the importance of AOEs – i.e., what proportion of variance in drinking do AOEs account for. Although some argue that AOEs can account for as much as 50% of the variance (see Del Boca and Darkes, 2001; Goldman et al., 1999), others (e.g., Jones et al., 2001) argue that proportion is actually much smaller, with an upper bound of 25% and a lower bound of 1-2%. This issue is particularly complex (and resolution is beyond the scope of this book) as there are multiple measures of AOEs and drinking behaviors and multiple strategies for data analysis. In addition, there are important questions about the measurement of AOEs. The majority of studies assess AOEs using self-report measures that draw upon more controlled, introspective, cognitive processes (see Thush and Wiers, 2007, for an exception); however, AOEs very likely have a strong automatic cognitive component which may better be assessed using alternative measures (e.g., implicit measures). Also related to the issue of measurement are findings that AOEs are context-specific. At least two studies have found differences in AOEs as a function of setting (a laboratory versus a college bar) (see Wall et al., 2000; Wall et al., 2001). These findings not only have implications for measurement but also for intervention efforts. Previous reviews have reached contradictory findings with respect to the efficacy of targeting AOEs for interventions (see Goldman et al., 1999; Jones et al., 2001) and increased construct and methodological clarity would likely be extremely useful.

Chapter 4

PROBLEM BEHAVIOR THEORY

Problem behavior theory (PBT) was initially proposed by Richard Jessor in the late 1960s (e.g., Jessor, Graves, Hanson, and Jessor, 1968) and revised to its most widely known form in the 1970s (e.g., Jessor and Jessor, 1977). PBT is a psychosocial and developmental approach for understanding problem behavior in adolescents and it has evolved over time. Because our treatment of PBT is necessarily brief, we refer interested readers elsewhere for more detailed descriptions (e.g., Jessor, 1987; 1998; Jessor, Donovan, and Costa, 1991; Jessor and Jessor, 1977). PBT is psychosocial and developmental in nature, and at its core, it suggests that the extent to which one engages in problem behaviors is predicted by one's "proneness to deviance," also called "unconventionality" (Donovan and Jessor, 1985; Jessor and Jessor, 1977). Deviance proneness is conceptualized as stemming from personality, perceived environmental, and behavioral systems. The former two are postulated to exert their influences both proximally and distally. PBT also proposes that each of the three systems is composed of variables that *instigate* or promote engaging in problem behaviors as well as variables that *control against* or inhibit engaging in problem behaviors. Ultimately, PBT holds that it is the *balance* of instigations and controls across these three systems that constitutes deviance proneness and predicts engagement in problem behaviors (Jessor, 1987).

What constitutes "problem behavior" in the eyes of PBT is contextual – i.e., problem behaviors are conceptualized to vary as a function of one's age and of current societal norms (Jessor, 1987; Jessor and Jessor, 1977). For example, consuming a single alcoholic beverage at age eight is a social norms transgression and thus, would be conceptualized as a problem behavior, whereas consuming a single alcoholic beverage at age 28 is not a social norms transgression, and thus would not be conceptualized as a problem behavior. Thus it is not necessarily engaging in a behavior, per se, that renders it problematic; often it is engaging in that behavior earlier than expected that renders the behavior problematic. Notably, PBT holds that deviance proneness leads to engagement in a broad constellation of problem behaviors (e.g., delinquency, alcohol use, problem drinking, tobacco use, illicit drug use, and early sexual behavior) rather than a single behavior or circumscribed set of behaviors. Thus, PBT holds that a single syndrome of problem behavior is predicted by the psychosocial construct of deviance proneness (Jessor and Jessor, 1977). This single syndrome has been proffered to explain the positive correlations in adolescents between a variety of behaviors such as alcohol use, tobacco use, illicit drug use, and sexual activity (e.g., Jessor, 1987). Finally, PBT also predicts that proneness to engage in problem behaviors is negatively associated with engagement in conventional behaviors (e.g., religious service attendance, school attendance, and other prosocial behaviors).

As stated above, PBT has evolved over time. The most recent formulation of PBT (e.g., Jessor, 1991) extended to health related behaviors. Parts of the 1991 reformulation were, in essence, semantic – i.e., the constructs of control agents have been reconceptualized as protective factors, and instigations have been reconceptualized as risk factors – in order to better match the terminology of health psychology and behavioral medicine. Thus, consistent with the earlier formulations, protective factors decrease the likelihood of engaging in a problem behavior and risk factors increase the likelihood of engaging in problem behavior. Some of the reformulation did go beyond semantics. Most importantly, protective factors (formerly control agents) were hypothesized to play an additional role. Not only were they predicted to decrease the likelihood of engaging in a problem behavior, but they were also predicted to moderate or attenuate the effect of exposure to risk factors (Jessor, 1991). In addition, the behavioral domain of the model has been expanded to include not only the prediction of problem behaviors but also the prediction of health behaviors and prosocial behaviors. Finally, in its modern form, PBT includes biology and genetics among its risk and protective factors (see Jessor, 1998), indicating that it may, ultimately, be better characterized as a bio-psycho-social-developmental model of risk behavior.

Because the focus of our book is on alcohol use, our review of the research findings will focus primarily on predictions and findings from PBT related to alcohol, with a brief discussion of the debate over whether problem behaviors do or do not represent a single syndrome. When used to predict adolescent alcohol use and problem drinking – the latter typically defined as a function of drinking to intoxication as well as having experienced at least one negative consequence from alcohol – PBT typically accounts for upwards of 30% of the variance (e.g., Costa, Jessor, and Turbin, 1999; Jessor, 1987; Hays, Stacy, and DiMatteo, 1987), with much of the variance explained by having friends who used alcohol and/or other substances. Similarly, when used to predict heavy episodic drinking in college students, risk and protective factors (as specified by the 1991 reformulation of PBT) accounted for approximately 25% of the variance after controlling for sociodemographic variables (Jessor, Costa, Krueger, and Turbin, 2006). Support has also been found for the role of protective factors as moderators of the effects of risk factors in both college (e.g., Jessor et al., 2006) and adolescent samples (Costa et al., 1999; Jessor et al., 1995). In addition, consistent with PBT, studies have also shown that deviant behaviors in adolescence predict drinking problems in adulthood (e.g., Clapper et al., 1995; DeCourville, 1995). Finally, PBT also hypothesizes that problem behaviors will be positively related to one another and negatively related to conventional behavior. In their study of six different samples of adolescents collected over a 20-year period, Donovan and colleagues (1999) reported results consistent with those predictions. Moreover, their findings indicated relatively consistent patterns of correlations among problem behaviors within and across each sample.

Research on PBT is characterized by several strengths. First, the studies tend to include large samples, typically ranging upwards of 800 (e.g., DeCourville, 1995; Jessor et al., 2006). Second, they tend to be longitudinal in nature, allowing for analysis related to transitioning into a problem behavior and maturing out of it. Some studies have also striven to recruit ethnically diverse samples (e.g., Costa et al., 1999), which allows for investigation of the generalizability of the model. Finally, as statistical methods and computer software packages have become more sophisticated and wide-spread, data analytic strategies have matured. Early tests of PBT tended to rely primarily on multiple correlation techniques (e.g., Jessor, 1987) whereas more recent studies have relied on more advanced statistics, including structural equation models, latent class models, and multidimensional scaling (e.g., Basen-Engquist et al., 1996; DeCourville, 1995; Willoughby et al., 2004).

Despite its strengths, PBT faces certain challenges both with respect to drinking, in particular, and to the model, more generally. Regarding the former, in PBT, problem behaviors are conceptualized as transgressions of norms. Although drinking under the age of 21 is illegal and a transgression in that sense, adolescent and young adult alcohol consumption is *statistically* normative (e.g., Baer et al., 1998; Johnston, O'Malley, Bachman, and Schulenberg, 2008, 2009). For example, more than half of 10th graders report having used alcohol in their lifetimes and more than half of 12th graders report having been drunk (Johnston et al., 2009); 72% of college students report having been drunk and 80% of young adults report having been drunk (Johnson et al., 2008). In addition, despite PBT's premise that problem behavior is a single syndrome, there have been contrary findings which suggest that multiple factors (vs. a single factor) may better fit the data (e.g., Basen-Engquist et al., 1996; Gillmore et al., 1991; Willoughby et al., 2004). In addition, others have found support for a single syndrome but, contrary to PBT, also found that problem behaviors were not negatively correlated with conventional behaviors (e.g., Farrell et al., 1992). Concerns have also been raised about the extent to which individual problem behaviors actually co-occur because of data analytic strategies that rely on correlations and therefore may not provide accurate predictions of the co-occurrence of problem behavior (Willoughby et al., 2004). Moreover, some studies that have tested the full PBT model have found that it did not fit the data as well as an abridged model (e.g., DeCourville, 1995). Finally, there is also mixed evidence with respect to PBT's generalizeabilty, with some studies finding it a better fit for White male adolescents from the U.S. than for Blacks or White females (e.g., Basen-Engquist et al., 1996) and others reporting a good fit for U.S. (Donovan et al., 1999; Jessor et al., 2003) and Chinese adolescents (Jessor et al., 2003).

SUMMARY AND IMPLICATIONS

PBT is a comprehensive psycho-social developmental theory for predicting adolescent problem behavior. Research findings indicate that its three systems (e.g., personality, perceived environment, and behavioral) explain a substantial amount of variance in alcohol use and problem drinking. Consistent with other social influence theories, findings testing PBT indicate the influence of friends and other models on drinking. Although not unique to PBT, such influences can be and often are targets for intervention. Unanswered questions with respect to PBT include the extent to which problem behaviors should or should not be conceptualized as a single syndrome. As discussed above, problem behaviors may better be conceptualized as several factors versus a single syndrome, and covariance among problem behaviors does not necessarily indicate co-occurrence. These issues have important treatment implications in terms of whether alcohol use should be targeted individually versus as a part of a larger constellation of maladaptive behaviors. Finally, generalizeabilty issues remain important concerns and future studies should continue to test PBT's applicability to populations beyond White American adolescents and young adults.

Chapter 5

SOCIAL COMPARISON THEORY

Social comparison theory was proposed by Leon Festinger in 1954. The original theory was formal and structured with nine hypotheses, eight corollaries, and eight deviations. The theory's basic premise is that people have a natural drive to evaluate themselves and, in the absence of objective criteria, compare themselves with other people. Much of the original theory considered with whom and on what dimensions people engage in social comparison. More than six decades of subsequent research (social comparison theory is cited in more than 3500 articles) has extended the theory considerably and most social influence theories acknowledge social comparison theory as an underlying foundation. Dimensions of social comparison that have been studied in detail include motivations for comparison, choice of comparison target, and effects of social comparison.

Although Festinger emphasized the desire to have an accurate self-evaluation as a motive, much subsequent research suggests that people also engage in social comparison as a means of self-improvement or ego-enhancement (Collins, 1996; Wills, 1981). Helgeson and Mickelson (1995) found direct support for the existence of these three motives, as well as three others (common bond, altruism, and self-destruction) by having participants list possible reasons why they themselves or anyone else might want to make social comparisons in response to a threatening event.

Choice of comparison target has also received extensive attention and overlaps with the literature evaluating motivations for engaging in social comparisons. Wills' (1981) downward comparison theory suggests that individuals may compare themselves with others who are of lower standing as a means of enhancing the self. Classic views suggested that lateral comparisons were motivated by accuracy whereas upward comparisons were motivated by self-improvement (Festinger, 1954; Wheeler, 1966). Subsequent research has shown that the specific choice of a comparison target, with respect to relative standing, is moderated by a number of situational and contextual variables, and there is no simple, general formula for the relationship between whom one compares with and why (e.g., Collins, 1996).

Similarly, the direction of comparison is associated with affect and esteem-related consequences. The traditional view (Suls and Wheeler, 2000) suggests that upward comparisons are most often associated with reduced positive affect, increased negative affect, and experienced as esteem-threatening. In contrast, downward comparisons are presumed most often associated with favorable affect and esteem-related outcomes. Here again, additional evidence has indicated that the impact of upward and downward comparisons are not so simple, and either direction can be associated with positive or negative consequences to the self, depending on context (Buunk, Collins, Taylor, VanYperen and Dakof, 1990; Collins, 1996).

Relatively little research has *formally* evaluated social comparison theory in the context of alcohol use. There have been at least four edited books dedicated to social comparison theory (Buunk and Gibbons, 1997; Stapel and Blanton, 2007; Suls and Wheeler, 2000; Suls and Wills, 1991), and only one of the included papers has a distinct alcohol focus. Stapel and Blanton (2007) include a reprint of a study in which Schroeder and Prentice (1998) evaluated pluralistic ignorance as a means of reducing drinking. Pluralistic ignorance and other constructs such as social norms (see Social Identity Theory) are implied and implicitly connected to social comparison theory but are not central to social comparison theory. Related, a compelling argument can be made that social comparison theory is the field in which many, if not most, perspectives related to social influence on alcohol are imbedded. For example, a considerable body of research has evaluated peer influences on adolescents, which are among the strongest predictors of adolescent substance use (e.g., Hawkins, Catalano, and Miller, 1992). Similarly, social norms are among the strongest influences of drinking among college students (Neighbors, Lee, Lewis, Fossos, and Larimer, 2007). Among young adults there is an extensive literature indicating strong peer influences on drinking generally and in specific situations (Borsari and Carey, 2001). Moreover, most conceptual-izations of peer influence require social comparisons as an integral part of the influence process. In order for others to have indirect influence on us (as opposed to direct requests to engage in a particular behavior), we must consider their expectations. Thus, on the one hand, it might be suggested that there are few studies focusing on social comparison and drinking among adolescents and young adults. However, on the other hand, it also might be suggested that there are few studies related to social influence on drinking in this population that are not related to social comparison theory.

Summary and implications. There are a number of promising directions for evaluating alcohol consumption in the context of social comparison theory. It would be worthwhile to reformulate existing findings related to peer social networks among adolescents, which are associated with drinking and other risk behaviors, in the context of social comparison theory (see review of Peer Cluster Theory). Examining social comparison processes as a function of maturation would provide ideas about how to tailor social influence approaches to prevention developmentally. In general, social comparison theory provides a rich theoretical foundation that is seldom formally evaluated in the context of drinking despite the potential practical implications for intervention development. We recommend more lab-based social comparison studies where alcohol use is used as the comparison dimension.

Chapter 6

SOCIAL IDENTITY THEORY

Social identity theory (SIT; Tajfel and Turner, 1986) describes the role of self-conception in relation to group membership, group processes, and intergroup relations. SIT was developed by Henri Tajfel in collaboration with John Turner. According to SIT and related theories, such as self-categorization theory (Turner, Hogg, Oakes, Reicher, and Wetherell, 1987), people view themselves and others as group members with a common or shared social identity, which is primarily comprised from group memberships. Individuals strive to maintain a positive social identity that is largely derived from positive comparisons between the in-group and relevant out-groups. SIT is composed of four primary elements: categorization, identification, comparison, and psychological distinctiveness. Categorization occurs when we place ourselves and others into categories, such as student, Asian, female, or fraternity member. The social category to which one belongs provides a definition of who one is based on the defining characteristics of the category (identification). People have a number of category memberships that vary in importance to the self, which serves to bolster self-esteem. Self-enhancement guides social categorization such that self-enhancement can be achieved by making comparisons between the in-group and relevant out-groups in ways that favor the in-group. Finally, psychological distinctiveness suggests that people desire to have a social identity that is distinct from yet positively compares with other groups.

Individuals have cognitive representations of social categories (i.e., prototypes) that consist of attributes that define one group and distinguish it from other groups. As such, category representations accentuate intragroup similarities and intergroup differences. Because prototypes tend to be shared by people within one group, they have group prototypes or group norms related to the in-group and relevant out-groups. In order for social categorization to influence normative behavior, categorization must be salient, such that individuals must psychologically identify with their in-group in the specific context. Thus, SIT proposes that norms and behaviors are tied to groups that are most salient (Christensen, Rothgerber, Wood, and Matz, 2004).

Although SIT as a whole has not been formally evaluated when applied to alcohol use, prior research examining alcohol use among adolescent and young adults has supported the notion that norms and behaviors are tied to salient referent groups. Several research studies have shown that normative perceptions of more proximal groups (e.g., same-sex peers, close friends), in comparison to more distal groups (e.g., typical student), are associated with alcohol use (Larimer et al., 2009; Lewis and Neighbors, 2004; Lewis, Neighbors, Oster-Aaland, Kirkeby, and Larimer, 2007; Yanovitsky, Stewart, and Lederman, 2006). For example, Larimer and colleagues (2009) evaluated whether descriptive drinking normative perceptions (i.e., the perceived prevalence of drinking behavior) varied based on specificity of the normative referent group at three levels (gender, race, and residence), and whether normative perceptions for more specific reference group norms were associated with alcohol consumption. Results indicated that participants distinguished between different referent groups when estimating descriptive drinking norms. Moreover, results demonstrated that perceived norms for more specific groups were uniquely related to participants' own alcohol consumption. Perceived norms at all three levels of specificity significantly added to the prediction of participants' own drinking, even when controlling for relevant covariates such as demographics and perceived norms for typical students.

Research conducted by Neighbors and colleagues (2009) found that the relationship between perceived descriptive drinking norms and alcohol consumption was moderated by level of identification with the normative referent (e.g., typical same-sex student, typical same-race student, and typical same-Greek status student). Findings indicated that when examining these relationships for all three normative referent groups, descriptive drinking normative perceptions for the normative referent were more strongly associated with alcohol consumption when participants reported feeling closer to (i.e., stronger identification with) the normative referent.

Similarly, Reed and colleagues (2007) evaluated the relationships among identity and perceived injunctive drinking norms (i.e., perceptions of how much others approve or accept of drinking behavior) for friends, other university peers, and Greek members. Results suggested that when these relationships were examined among friends, perceived injunctive drinking norms were positively associated with consuming more drinks per occasion, and that was especially true as identification with friends increased. For other university peers, identification was associated with drinking only for those who perceived other university students as more approving of drinking behavior (medium and high levels of approval). For Greek normative referents, identification was associated with drinking only for those who perceived Greek members as strongly approving of drinking behavior. Together, findings from Larimer and colleagues (2009), Neighbors and colleagues (2009), and Reed and colleagues (2007) support SIT such that the relationship between both perceived descriptive and injunctive normative drinking behavior with alcohol consumption may depend on how strongly students identify with the normative referent.

SIT's concept that categorization must be salient in order to influence normative behavior has also been applied to social norms interventions for adolescent and young adult alcohol use. Universal social norms marketing interventions (e.g., DeJong et al., 2006; Perkins and Craig, 2006; Perkins, Haines, and Rice, 2005) attempt to correct overestimated normative perceptions for relevant peer groups by presenting accurate norms messages on a large scale (e.g., 85% of students on this campus drink 0-1-2-3 or at most 4 drinks when they party), often through campus newspaper ads, emails, posters, and/or flyers. Research on social norms marketing has produced equivocal support. Some findings demonstrate support for social norms marketing as an effective intervention for reducing alcohol consumption (e.g., DeJong et al., 2006; Mattern and Neighbors, 2004; Perkins and Craig, 2006; Perkins et al., 2005) and other research concludes partial or no support (e.g., Clapp, Lange, Russell, Shillington, and Voas, 2003; Thombs and Hamilton, 2002; Wechsler, Lee, Nelson, and Lee, 2003; Werch et al., 2000).

Personalized normative feedback is also a social norms approach to reducing alcohol use, which attempts to correct overestimated normative misperceptions by presenting individual feedback regarding the student's own drinking, the student's perception of others' drinking, and others' actual drinking (Lewis and Neighbors, 2007; Lewis, Neighbors, Oster-Aaland, Kirkeby, and Larimer, 2007; Neighbors, Larimer, and Lewis, 2004; Neighbors, Lewis, Bergstrom, and Larimer, 2006). Personalized intervention strategies using normative comparisons have generally yielded promising results showing reductions in normative perceptions of peer drinking and reductions in drinking behavior (Carey, Scott-Sheldon, Carey, DeMartini, 2007; Larimer and Cronce, 2002, 2007; Walters and Neighbors, 2005).

Many personalized feedback interventions have incorporated other components, such as review of risk factors, expectancy challenge, and blood alcohol concentration information (Carey et al., 2007; Larimer and Cronce, 2002, 2007); thus evaluation of single component personalized feedback interventions are necessary. A handful of studies have evaluated the effects of personalized normative feedback as a single component intervention (Lewis and Neighbors, 2007; Lewis, Neighbors et al., 2007; Neighbors et al., 2004; Neighbors et al., 2006). These studies have all demonstrated that personalized normative feedback is effective at reducing normative perceptions and drinking behavior. When examining personalized normative feedback in relation to SIT, Lewis and Neighbors (2007) evaluated gender-nonspecific and gender-specific versions of a brief personalized normative feedback intervention aimed at reducing alcohol consumption among college students. Consistent with SIT, findings indicated that gender-specific personalized normative feedback was especially effective at reducing drinking for women who more strongly identified with their gender at a two-month follow-up.

SUMMARY AND IMPLICATIONS

According to SIT, adolescents and young adults form social identities based on group membership, or categorization. Identification with in-groups, and comparison with in-groups and relevant out-groups aid in making these social identities distinct for individuals. Aspects of SIT have been applied to etiology and prevention research. Specifically, salience of the in-group is often a moderator of the relationship between social norms and alcohol use. For example, prior research has demonstrated that more closely identifying with relevant normative referents is associated with increased normative perceptions for drinking behavior as well as increased personal alcohol use. In addition, research evaluating preventative interventions has found that personalized normative feedback is more effective in certain instances when identification with the normative referent is stronger. Additional research is needed to extend these findings to adolescent and non-college young adult populations.

Chapter 7

SELF-DEROGATION THEORY

Self-derogation theory is a broad theory that describes the interplay between socialization factors, self-esteem, deviant behavior, and associations with deviant peers (Kaplan, 1982; 1987; 2001). The theory suggests, among adolescents, a number of factors may contribute to the development of low self-esteem, self-rejection, and rejection of the norms and values endorsed by the broader society. These factors, in turn, may motivate adolescents to engage in deviant behaviors, including alcohol and drug use, and seek out similarly deviant peers. Under these circumstances, involvement with and acceptance by deviant peers provides a means of restoring or enhancing an adolescent's sense of self-worth.

A number of social, familial, cultural, and intrapersonal factors have been proposed to increase the likelihood of self-rejection (i.e., self-derogation; Kaplan, 2001). These include peer rejection, parental neglect and poor family cohesion, academic failure, stigmatization, and inadequate coping skills, among others. Adolescents who feel disenfranchised from conventional society and who do not fit in with main stream peers lose motivation to conform to societal norms. They may respond with reactance and rejection of conventional values (see Reactance Theory) whereby they engage in deviant behaviors. In other words, having failed to fit in with the main stream, these adolescents engage in deviant behaviors as an alternative response pattern. They may concurrently seek out others who have similarly rejected conventional norms (see Peer Cluster Theory), which is predicted to increase deviant behaviors and self-worth.

The model is difficult to test in its entirety because it is a process model and requires longitudinal data spanning the period of adolescence. The breadth of the theory provides considerable overlap with other theoretical perspectives and bodies of research regarding risk and protective factors (Hawkins, Catalano, and Miller, 1992; also see Problem Behavior Theory) as well as peer influences on alcohol and other substance use (Oetting and Beauvais, 1987). For example, a considerable body of evidence supports associations between family factors (e.g., attachment, parental support, parental monitoring, and family conflict) and alcohol and other substance use (Bray, Adams, Getz, and Baer, 2001; Petraitis, Flay and Miller, 1995).

The relationship between self-esteem and alcohol has been somewhat mixed although higher self-esteem has been prospectively associated with less alcohol and other substance use in adolescence (Stein, Newcomb, and Bentler, 1987). In college students, morally-based self-esteem, and esteem based on God's love, has been associated with less drinking (Lewis, Phillipi, and Neighbors, 2007; Luhtanen and Crocker, 2005) whereas self-esteem based on appearance has been associated with increased drinking (Luhtanen and Crocker, 2005). More central to the theory are how self-esteem, peer associations, and deviant behaviors are associated over time.

Mason (2001) found direct support for this aspect of self-derogation theory, finding delinquency to be associated with growth in self-esteem among adolescent boys who were initially low in self-esteem. The measure of delinquency did not however include alcohol and other substance use. More recently, in a longitudinal sample of American Indian adolescents, Radin and colleagues (2006) found that low self-worth was associated with alcohol-related problems and that this relationship was mediated by associations with deviant peers in earlier, but not later adolescence. In later adolescence self-esteem and peer deviance had direct associations with alcohol-related problems. Using latent growth analysis, Radin and colleagues also found some support for a comprehensive model of self-derogation theory. Specifically, family cohesion, family conflict, and academic competence were associated with initial self-worth and changes in self-worth in expected directions. Self-worth and increases in self-worth were associated with lower peer deviance. Peer deviance and changes in peer deviance were, in turn, associated with drinking and changes in drinking. Thus, risk factors were associated with lower self-worth, which was in turn, associated with peer deviance and subsequent alcohol use. Radin and colleagues (2006) did not, however, find any support for affiliation with deviant peers having positive effects on changes in self-worth.

SUMMARY AND IMPLICATIONS

Self-derogation theory shares a number of commonalities with other theories of social influence (e.g., Problem Behavior Theory, Reactance Theory and Peer Cluster Theory) but also makes some unique predictions regarding the potential incentives of substance use and affiliation with other substance users among adolescents who feel rejected from conventional society. The theory's primary implications for intervention are in the identification of risk factors and potential issues to be addressed among deviant adolescents. The theory has been primarily examined in adolescents and is presumed to be most relevant to this time period. However, future research examining the potential long term affects of self-derogation into young adulthood would be worthwhile.

Chapter 8

THEORY OF REASONED ACTION AND THEORY OF PLANNED BEHAVIOR

The theory of reasoned action, developed by Ajzen and Fishbein (TRA; Ajzen and Fishbein, 1980; Fishbein and Ajzen, 1975), was designed to predict and explain human behavior in specific contexts. This theory suggests that behavior is determined by intentions to perform the behavior, and that intentions are a function of attitudes toward the behavior and subjective norms toward the behavior. Ajzen extended the TRA to the theory of planned behavior (TPB; Ajzen, 1988, 1991) such that perceived behavioral control, together with behavioral intentions, can be used directly to predict behavior.

According to the TRA and the TPB, the best predictor of a behavior is intention to engage in that behavior. Thus, intentions are considered to be the immediate antecedent of reasoned and planned behavior. Intentions are determined by attitudes toward the specific behavior (i.e., beliefs about consequences or attributes of the behavior), subjective norms toward the specific behavior (i.e., beliefs about how important others will view the specific behavior), and perceived behavioral control (i.e., one's perceptions of their ability to perform a given behavior). An assumption of these theories is that the more favorable the attitude and the subjective norm, and the greater the perceived behavioral control, the stronger the intentions to perform the behavior. Furthermore, the stronger the intention to engage in a behavior, the more likely one will do so. According the TPB, behavioral intentions are only predictive of behavior when the behavior is perceived as being under one's volitional control (i.e., if the person can decide to engage or not engage in the behavior).

Armitage and Connor (2001) reviewed the research on the TPB and found that across studies the TPB accounted for 27% to 39% of the variance in behavior and intentions, respectively. In addition, they found that the subjective norm construct was generally a weaker predictor of intentions in comparison to attitudes and perceived behavioral control, which was in part due to poor measurement and the need to expand the subjective norm component of the model. When applied specifically to adolescent and young adult alcohol use, both the TRA and the TPB are empirically supported (Connor, Warren, Close, and Sparks,1999; Collins and Carey, 2007; Huchting, Lac, and LaBrie, 2008; Johnston and White, 2003; Kam, Matsunaga, Hecht, and Ndiaye, 2009; Kuther and Higgens-D'Alessandro, 2003; Marcoux and Shope, 1997; McMillan and Connor, 2003; Norman, Armitage, and Quigley, 2007; Norman and Conner, 2006; O'Callaghan, Chant, Callan, and Baglioni, 1996; Schlegal, D'Avernas, Zanna, DeCourville, and Manske, 1992).

However, despite the empirical support of the TRA and the TPB when applied to alcohol use among adolescents and young adults, as well as across a wide range of other behaviors, a major shortcoming of these models is their inability to account fully for the influence of past behavior on alcohol use intentions and future alcohol use. Prior research has shown that past behavior is one of the strongest predictors of intentions and future behavior, explaining variance over and above that accounted for by the TPB variables (Ajzen, 1991; Conner and Armitage, 1998; Ouellette and Wood, 1998). For example, Conner and Armitage (1998) reported that the addition of past behavior to the TPB variables explains, on average, an additional 7% of the variance in intention and 13% of the variance in behavior.

Recent research has examined the role of past behavior in the TPB. For example, Collins and Carey (2007) examined the TPB in an undergraduate student sample, and found that self-efficacy and attitudes significantly predicted intentions, and that intentions to engage in heavy-episodic drinking predicted future heavy-episodic drinking. However, subjective norms were not found to be predictive of intentions. Findings further indicated that a model including past heavy-episodic drinking did not provide a better fit than the model excluding past behavior. The authors concluded that a TPB model excluding past behavior, which is more parsimonious and theory driven, may provide better prediction of heavy-episodic drinking among college drinkers than a model including past behavior.

Norman and Conner (2006) examined the TPB in relation to heavy-episodic drinking among college students. Findings indicated that attitude, self-efficacy, and perceived control were predictive of heavy-episodic drinking intentions. Findings indicated the TPB to be predictive of intentions to engage in heavy-episodic drinking over the next week, explaining an additional 66% of the variance in intentions when controlling for age and gender. Attitude, self-efficacy, and perceived control were significant predictors. Furthermore, results indicated that additional variance was explained by past behavior, and that past behavior moderated the associations between attitude and intention and intentions and behavior. Weaker relationships were found as frequency of past behavior increased. The authors explained that this finding is consistent with the idea that repeatedly performing a behavior leads to a reduction in the amount of deliberative processing, and thus, attitudes are less important when determining intentions as the frequency of past behavior increases. Similarly, intentions become less important in determining behavior as the frequency of past behavior increases. Thus, while research has examined the role of past behavior in relation to the TRA and the TPB, findings are mixed as to whether including past behavior enhances the predictability of these two models.

SUMMARY AND IMPLICATIONS

According to the TRA and the TPB, alcohol use among adolescents and young adults is predicted by intentions to use alcohol, which are predicted by attitudes toward alcohol, subjective norms related to alcohol, and perceived behavioral control. The results of the above studies confirm the predictive validity of the TPB in relation to alcohol-related intentions and behavior among adolescents and young adults. Furthermore, research literature on the TRA and the TPB suggest that preventative interventions should target favorable attitudes toward alcohol use, such as alcohol-expectancy challenge interventions (for a review see Carey et al., 2007; Larimer and Cronce, 2002; 2007). In addition, perceived subjective norms for alcohol use should be targeted. Prior research has shown that subjective norms are often misperceived such that adolescents and young adults perceive important others' as more approving of alcohol use than they actually are (Borsari and Carey, 2001; Carey, Borsari, Carey, and Maisto, 2006; Suls and Green, 2003). Providing accurate subjective normative information for alcohol use may reduce perceived approval of alcohol use, and in turn lower intentions and behavior. Finally, preventative interventions could provide skills aimed at increasing drinking-refusal self-efficacy (for a review see Carey et al., 2007; Larimer and Cronce, 2002; 2007).

Chapter 9

PROTOTYPE/WILLINGNESS MODEL

The prototype/willingness model is used to explain complex health behaviors in adolescents and young adults. (Gerrard, Gibbons, Houlihan, Stock, and Pomery, 2008; Gibbons, Gerrard, Blanton, and Russell, 1998), and is based on theories of social cognition and primarily draws from the TRA. The prototype-willingness model is a dual-processing model that posits that there are two related yet independent paths, a reasoned path and a social reaction path, to risky health behaviors for adolescents and young adults. The reasoned path represents a deliberative style of processing, similar to that proposed in the theory of reasoned action. Within this path, actions are premeditated and planned (analytic processing) and are a function of behavioral intentions. Attitudes and subjective norms toward the behavior predict intentions. In contrast, the social reaction path represents a different style of processing, one that is more heuristic-based or experiential (heuristic processing). This pathway of the model suggests that there are times (more so for adolescents) when behavior is unintended, and is rather less deliberative and often occurs from being in situations that facilitate risky behaviors. Once in these risky situations, it is not reasoned decision making (behavioral intentions), but behavioral willingness that determines behavior. Risk prototypes (e.g., the typical drinker) and behavioral willingness (i.e., an openness to engaging in risky behavior) are two key components of the social reaction path. Behavioral willingness predicts behavior, and is a function of risk images or prototypes. Unlike the TRA, previous behavior is included in the model as a predictor of attitudes, subjective norms, and risk images.

There are several basic assumptions of the prototype/willingness model. One basic assumption is that adolescent and young adult health risk behavior is usually volitional (their choice), but is often not planned or even intentional. Prior research has shown that adolescents and young adults who engaged in a risky behavior, will have previously reported no intention to engage in that risky behavior in the future (Gibbons et al., 1998). Gerrard and colleagues (2008) suggest that this discrepancy between intentions and behavior is not due to misrepresentation of intentions but rather is a reflection of images of who engages in drinking behavior.

A second major assumption of the prototype/willingness model is that adolescents and young adults have distinct social images or cognitive representations (prototypes) of the type of person their age who engages in specific risk behaviors (typology of a person rather than a description). These social images or prototypes are associated with behavioral willingness, such that the more favorable the image of a drinker, the more likely they are to engage in alcohol use and to accept the social consequences of being seen as a drinker. Prior research has supported the social reaction path of the prototype/willingness model when applied to adolescent and young adult alcohol use (Andrews, Hampson, Barchley, Gerrard, and Gibbons, 2008; Blanton, Gibbons, Gerrard, Conger, and Smith, 1997; Gerrard et al., 2002; Rivis, Sheeran, and Armitage, 2006; Spijkerman, van den Eijnden, Vitale, and Engels, 2004). For example, Andrews and colleagues (2008) found that adolescents' prototypes of drinkers were either indirectly related to alcohol use through willingness or were directly related to alcohol use.

An additional assumption of the prototype/willingness model is that the relationship between intentions and behavior becomes stronger than the relationship between willingness and behavior over time. Thus, as adolescents and young adults age and become more experienced, decision making tends to shift from a more reactive process (social reaction path) to a more reasoned one (reasoned path). Although this assumption has not yet been tested when applied to adolescent and young adult alcohol use, it has been supported in various other high-risk behaviors including condom use, smoking, and skipping class (Gerrard et al., 2008).

Finally, according to the prototype/willingness model, prototypes are easier to change when younger, and specifically in those who do not engage in the risk behavior. Thus, change is more likely before the development of prototypes and a stable behavior pattern. Interventions designed to change prototype images at an early age are likely to be effective in decreasing willingness to engage in alcohol use, and subsequently alcohol use (Gerrard et al., 2006). When evaluated among adolescents, Gerrard and colleagues (2006) found support for a prototype-willingness model based intervention. This study examined a dual-focus prevention intervention aimed to delay the onset of alcohol use and to reduce alcohol consumption among African American adolescents. Findings indicated that two-years following the intervention, changes in alcohol consumption were mediated by two paths, the reasoned path and the social reaction path. The reasoned path demonstrated that the intervention influenced intentions to drink by increasing parenting behaviors related to alcohol. The social reaction path provided evidence that the intervention decreased willingness to drink by decreasing the favorability of drinker images. Furthermore, changes in intentions and willingness were independently associated with alcohol consumption at the two-year follow-up. The authors suggest that taking a dual-process approach to preventative interventions that targets both intentions and willingness is likely to be more effective than targeting either alone.

Although change in alcohol use becomes more difficult as prototypes develop and as individuals have more experiences or stable patterns of alcohol use, it may still be possible to alter drinker images and change drinking behavior into adulthood. For example, Gibbons and colleagues (2005) found that among college students and young adults that interventions can reduce the favorability of the image of a sun bather or typical person who uses a tanning booth, and thus reduce willingness to be exposed to UV rays. Interventions applying the prototype/willingness model still need to be evaluated for reducing alcohol use among young adults.

SUMMARY AND IMPLICATIONS

The prototype/willingness model is a dual-process model that incorporates a reasoned, intentional approach to predicting behavior as well as a more reactive approach to predicting behavior. Research has provided support for these two pathways in predicting alcohol use in adolescents and young adults. Moreover, research has shown that prevention interventions aimed at reducing intentions and willingness to drink are effective in reducing drinking in adolescents. Additional research is needed to replicate these findings in preventing and/or reducing drinking in young adults.

Chapter 10

DEVIANCE REGULATION THEORY

Developed by Blanton and colleagues, Deviance regulation theory (DRT; Blanton, Stuart, and VandenEijnden, 2001; Blanton and Christie, 2003) presents a novel perspective on social influence. While most theories of social influence assume that conformity lies at the root of social influence, DRT suggests that deviance, rather than conformity, is a more central motivator. This theory offers the compelling rationale that it is what makes us different that defines us, to ourselves, and to others. More specifically, DRT suggests that individuals attempt to maintain positive images by seeking to deviate from social norms in a positive way and by avoiding deviation from social norms that are viewed negatively. Consistent with classic attribution perspectives (Jones and Davis, 1965; Kelley, 1967) the theory suggests that distinctive actions (i.e., counter-normative alternatives) receive greater weight in impression formation and are therefore most strongly considered in the regulation of social behaviors. In essence, behaving the same way everyone else does has little impact on one's social identity. Rather, it is when behavior is distinctive that others alter their impressions of themselves which, in turn, has implications for their personal identity and sense of self-worth (Leary, Tambor, Terdal, and Downs, 1995). Distinctiveness can be either positive or negative depending on the prevailing attitudes and values of the self and the reference group. For example, being the only person not drinking alcohol at a keg party may result in negative social distinction. Similarly, excessive drinking at a formal social gathering where few people are drinking is also likely to constitute negative social distinction.

Blanton, Stuart, and VandenEijnden (2001) conducted several experiments testing hypotheses derived from DRT. In one of these studies they randomly assigned participants to receive information suggesting that getting a flu shot was normative (i.e., most students get flu shots) or non-normative (i.e., few students get flu shots). Some students received positively framed persuasive messages (i.e., getting a flu shot is good) whereas others received negatively framed persuasive messages (i.e., not getting a flu shot is bad). Consistent with their theoretical framework, the two conditions that were most strongly associated with intentions to get a flu shot were the normative negatively framed condition (i.e., most students get flu shots and not getting a flu shot is bad) and the non-normative positively framed condition (i.e., few students get flu shots and getting a flu shot is good). In another one of these studies they found the identical pattern regarding willingness to have unprotected sex. In this study Blanton and colleagues (2001) measured participants' perceived norms regarding condom use and then, two weeks later, exposed them to either positively framed messages (using condoms is good) or negatively framed messages (not using condoms is bad). Students who believed condom use was relatively rare were most unwilling to have unprotected sex when they were exposed to positively framed messages. Students who believed condom use was relatively common were most unwilling to engage in unprotected sex when they received negatively framed messages.

DRT also suggests that inferences about prevalence are made on the basis of how messages are framed. For example, Stuart and Blanton (2003) found that prevalence estimates for condom use were higher among participants who were exposed to a negatively framed message (i.e., having sex without a condom is stupid) compared with participants who were exposed to a positively framed message (i.e., using condoms is smart). Thus, according to DRT, just as prevalence estimates influence the impact of positively versus negatively framed messages (Blanton et al., 2001), positively versus negatively framed messages influence prevalence estimates.

Although no published empirical research to date has directly evaluated DRT in the context of alcohol use, there have been speculations regarding its applicability to norms based alcohol interventions for adolescents (Blanton and Burkley, 2008) and college students (Blanton, Koblitz, and McCaul, 2008). In the context of discussing DRT's application to adolescents, Blanton and Burkley (2008) describe an unpublished study examining the effects of exposure to positively versus negatively framed messages about healthy drinking on college students' drinking intentions. They reported that negatively framed messages reduced drinking intentions among students with little drinking history, as would be expected assuming these students are more likely to believe healthy drinking is the norm and that unhealthy drinking is a negative behavior. They further reported that, among students with extensive drinking backgrounds, exposure to negatively framed messages was not only ineffective, but was iatrogenic, increasing drinking intentions. Assuming these students were more likely to believe that drinking is good and common, this finding would not support DRT, but would be more consistent with suggestions that heavy drinking students may be more defensive and reactive to pejorative alcohol statements (Neighbors, Palmer, and Larimer, 2004). Thus, while preliminary evidence suggests this theory may be applicable to drinking, it may be more applicable to universal prevention and messages to adolescents and/or young adults who have a limited drinking history.

SUMMARY AND IMPLICATIONS

The primary limitation of DRT is the relatively small number of studies evaluating hypotheses derived from the theory. Perhaps more importantly, none of the published studies to date have evaluated the impact of messages on actual behavior change but have been limited to studying intentions or willingness to engage in health-related behaviors. Thus, to date, there is no efficacy data for prevention/intervention strategies derived from this theory. Moreover, it has yet to be explored in detail in the context of alcohol use. In contrast, DRT has a number of appealing characteristics which make it worthy of inclusion. It is one of the most novel and innovative perspectives on social influence to be offered in recent years. Whether correct or incorrect, the theory offers clear straight forward and theoretically rich hypotheses about how to frame alcohol interventions for adolescents and young adults. Current approaches to alcohol interventions, understandably, tend to emphasize what works in changing behavior often at the expense of theoretical innovation. However, the ability to continue to develop new and better approaches for interventions rests on theoretical innovation, and DRT is a promising candidate.

Chapter 11

PEER CLUSTER THEORY

Peer cluster theory, first introduced by Oetting and Beauvais (1986), is a psychosocial model that proposes that socialization factors associated with adolescent development interact to create peer clusters that either support or discourage alcohol and other substance use. The peer cluster, different from the broader and more loosely associated peer group, is a small and cohesive unit of friends that serves as the dominant sphere of influence, that shapes adolescent behavior (Oetting and Beauvais, 1987). While peer cluster theory recognizes other factors in the adolescent social network that either increase or decrease the probability of alcohol and drug involvement, these elements only indirectly affect substance use to the extent that they influence the selection of a peer cluster (Oetting and Lynch, 2006). More specifically, this theory identifies several psychosocial characteristics that motivate drug use, including social structure, socialization links, and psychological characteristics. Again, these factors only lay the groundwork for the formation of either a substance-using or a substance-abstaining peer cluster (Oetting and Beauvais, 1986). Moreover, it is primarily peer clusters that "shape and determine attitudes, values, and beliefs about drugs…and, to a great extent, determine the actual drug-taking behaviors (Oetting and Beauvais, 1987)."

According to peer cluster theory, in order to successfully treat a substance-abusing adolescent, the counselor must first separate the individual from his or her substance-using peer cluster. The counselor must also address the original psychosocial elements that established the vulnerability to substance involvement. If these elements remain strong in the adolescent's life, then the adolescent remains susceptible. Peer cluster theory posits that alcohol and drug treatment approaches that do not stress changes in peer associations first and foremost, will ultimately, be ineffective (Oetting and Beauvais 1986).

In their study of 415 eleventh and twelfth grade students, Oetting and Beauvais (1987) confirmed two of their primary hypotheses about socialization characteristics and substance use. The first of these hypotheses was that socialization characteristics are significantly correlated with substance use, indicating that theories of substance use should not neglect the influence of psychosocial characteristics. The second hypothesis, supported by the results of this study, was that peer substance associations were preeminent among psychosocial factors predicting adolescent substance use. The results of Swaim, Oetting, Edwards and Beauvais' (1989) study of 563 high school students similarly indicated that peer substance associations were highly predictive of adolescent substance use. Moreover, emotional distress was found to be associated with substance use only indirectly through peer substance use. Finally, Bray, Adams, Getz, and McQueen (2003) investigated patterns of adolescent alcohol use in their longitudinal study of 6,048 students in the Southwestern United States. Among the goals of the study was to examine the relationship between peer alcohol use and adolescent alcohol use. Results of this study mirrored those in the previously mentioned two studies: peer alcohol use influenced youth drinking. Additionally, findings of this research emphasized the importance of studying the longitudinal relationships between peer alcohol use and youth alcohol consumption, while also taking into consideration the capacity for change and growth.

Related to peer cluster theory, in the prevention domain, social resistance skills training has been an effective component of many empirically supported primary prevention strategies (Botvin, 2000). Similarly, building efficacy for social resistance has been incorporated in empirically supported treatments for alcohol (e.g., Marlatt and Donovan, 2005). Both domains acknowledge the powerful influence of close peers on alcohol and other substance use and provide practical strategies for resisting this influence.

SUMMARY AND IMPLICATIONS

In sum, peer cluster theory stresses the strong influence of close peers on the use of alcohol and other substances, especially among adolescents and further suggests the value of incorporating some aspect of the peer cluster into alcohol interventions. Peer cluster theory has important implications for interventions targeting adolescent and young adult alcohol use. Peer cluster theory suggests interventions centering solely on the individual, and neglecting the social network, will be ineffective. Small group interventions targeting either the peer cluster directly or incorporating supportive peers in interventions are a natural extension of peer cluster theory. Some concerns have been raised regarding the potential for high-risk peers to influence one another negatively in adolescent group interventions (Dishion, McCord, and Poulin, 1999), however a meta-analysis examining the validity of this concern revealed little support (Weiss et al., 2005). More recently, Tevyaw, Borsari, Colby, and Monti (2007) evaluated a peer enhanced brief motivational intervention and found support for the inclusion of peers in targeting alcohol use among college students. Specifically, relative to an individual brief motivational intervention, a brief motivational intervention with a supportive friend present resulted in greater reductions in drinking and alcohol related problems and higher satisfaction ratings. Future studies might also explore individual-centered interventions that seek to incorporate friends, who are part of the alcohol-using peer cluster.

Chapter 12

REACTANCE THEORY

Reactance theory (RT) was formulated in the 1960s (Brehm, 1966), and suggests that reducing or threatening to reduce a person's freedom will result in arousal – so-called "motivational arousal." RT further argues that people are motivated to reestablish or regain their freedoms through non-compliance. Psychological reactance is, therefore, a motivational *state* that leads people to remove threats to their freedom, regain their freedom, and prevent such threats from occurring again. The original formulation of RT specifies that reactance is best understood as a state versus a trait (Brehm, 1966). Others have argued that reactance could also be understood as an individual difference variable, suggesting that some people may be more reactant than others, and much of that research has sought methods to identify and intervene with "reactant" clients or patients (Beutler et al., 1991; Dillard and Shen, 2005; Shoham-Salomon and Hannah, 1991). This view of RT as a trait is controversial and inconsistent with the original formulation of RT, and findings are mixed, at best (see Shoham, Trost, and Rohrbaugh, 2004). Accordingly, the present review will limit its scope to (a) consideration of RT as a state and (b) RT's application to adolescent and young adult alcohol use.

It would seem that RT would have substantial application to alcohol research, in general – (e.g., intervention and prevention efforts can be considered to be attempts to reduce a person's freedom to drink) and to alcohol research on adolescents and young adults in particular (e.g., in the U.S. a myriad of legal and public health efforts have been launched at restricting or limiting adolescents and young adults' access to, consumption of, and consequences from alcohol). In addition, adolescents and young adults are thought to be, from a developmental perspective, at a period in their lives in which rebellion and questioning authority are normative (see Arnett, 2000). Surprisingly, little research formally tests RT with respect to alcohol use. Instead, most research seems either to capitalize on opportunities for naturalistic studies (e.g., changes in drinking laws) or to offer RT as a possible post hoc explanation for study findings or survey trends. There appears to be a recent resurgence of interest in RT within the field of health communication, which may presage additional research within alcohol studies.

With respect to naturalistic studies, two changes in laws – one raising the minimum age for purchase and public possession to 21 and the second requiring warning labels on alcoholic beverages – provided opportunities to investigate whether restrictions on young adults' and adolescents' freedom to drink would result in more drinking as a means of restoring that freedom. In both instances, findings have been mixed. Related to the former, two studies of students at post-secondary school institutions (e.g., colleges, community colleges, technical schools, etc.) have been conducted. One found that students who were not of legal age consumed more than students who were of age and that a higher percentage of students underage were drinkers as compared to students who were of age (Engs and Hanson, 1989). A second found more drinking among students who were not of age as compared to those who were but no difference in the use of illicit drugs among students who were and were not of legal drinking age (arguably because there were no recent or new changes in laws regulating them) (Allen, Sprenkel, and Vitale, 1994). In contrast, however, at least two studies found that drinking did not change substantially either one month (e.g., Gordon and Minor, 1992) or one year (e.g., Perkins and Berkowitz, 1989) after changes to the minimum purchase age went into effect. Gordon and Minor (1992), however, argued that those underage "needed time" to regain their lost freedom to drink and examined another group 13 months after the law change. Although they found an increase in drinking, it is unclear if that finding is due to method effects – e.g., the study asked specifically and directly about alcohol consumption before and after the law change, possibly creating strong demand characteristics. Similar to findings related to changing the purchase age, warning label findings have been equivocal, suggesting, at best, that the labels neither increase nor decrease consumption (see Andrews, 1995; MacKinnon, Nohre, Cheong, and Stacy, 2001).

Beyond changes in law, RT has also been considered in light of the recent emphasis on social norms marketing approaches to alcohol education and prevention (e.g., DeJong et al., 2006 see also Social Identity Theory). In particular, it has been suggested that social norms marketing campaigns may "misfire" or "boomerang" and create reactance among (heavier) drinking adolescents and young adults (e.g., Cameron and Campo, 2006; Campo and Cameron, 2006). A study by Campo and Cameron (2006) found some support for college-wide social norms marketing campaigns resulting in more negative health attitudes about one's own drinking (e.g., being less likely to endorse that "drinking to get drunk is a bad idea") and that more such attitudes were more likely to occur in the heaviest drinkers. Similarly, a study of an Australian government-backed alcohol campaign, which essentially targeted injunctive norms about drinking and drinking-related consequences, found that although many college students liked the campaign and thought it was effective, other students were very negative about it (e.g., Ricciardelli and McCabe, 2008). The authors suggested that many of the negative remarks were consistent with RT – e.g., students do not want to be told what to do or do not care or will drink regardless. A significant limitation of the aforementioned studies, however, is that none assessed pre-, post, or follow-up drinking *behaviors*.

Within the field of health communications more broadly, there has been some experimental work as to what makes health-oriented messages (some of which were alcohol-related) more persuasive and less likely to elicit reactance (e.g., Dillard and Shen, 2005; Miller, Lane, Deatrick, Young, and Potts, 2007; Rains and Turner, 2007). Consistent with RT, findings suggest that (a) more controlling messages are perceived negatively by college students and (b) "restorative" postscripts, which remind readers that it is their choice whether or not to follow the message's advice, are perceived positively (Miller et al., 2007). In addition, another study suggests that a smaller sized request is also associated with less reactance (Rains and Turner, 2007). However, none of the aforementioned studies included post-tests or follow up assessments of actual drinking or other health behaviors.

SUMMARY AND IMPLICATIONS

Ultimately, findings are mixed with respect to RT, and even studies with findings supportive of RT typically cannot rule out alternative interpretations or make claims about changes in actual behavior due to methodological limitations. Moreover, recent studies seem to focus exclusively on college students; thus, the implications for adolescents and young adults not attending college are unclear. However, the recent resurgence in the health communication literature is promising; it is hoped that future studies will continue to assess messages about alcohol consumption, to go beyond college populations and to measure and link RT directly to drinking behavior and consequences. Moreover, findings from those studies suggest that some current alcohol intervention strategies (e.g., motivational interviewing: Miller and Rollnick, 1991, 2002) may be particularly useful because (a) therapists specifically tell clients that they can choose not to change (i.e., retain their freedom to drink) and (b) therapists are instructed to avoid eliciting resistance and defensiveness and to change tactics immediately if either occurs. In addition, given the likelihood that the most extreme college drinkers are less likely to attend drinking interventions (see Neighbors, Palmer, and Larimer, 2004), it seems vitally important for continued and more methodologically rigorous research on reactance theory and alcohol use.

Chapter 13

CONCLUSION

As reviewed within this book, there are a number of theoretical models that place importance on social influence in relation to decision making and behavior. Specifically, this book reviewed theories of social influence in relation to etiology and prevention of adolescent and young adult alcohol use. One criterion of success of a psychological theory is its explanatory, predictive, and generative power. A key to preventing alcohol use and associated negative consequences in adolescents and young adults is gaining understanding as to why individuals initiate and continue to engage in those behaviors. Thus, when applied to alcohol use, a successful theory can explain alcohol use, predict alcohol use, and provide a basis for innovation to produce additional empirical research. Some of the theories reviewed in this book had more explanatory, predictive, and generative power when applied to the etiology of adolescent and young adult alcohol use, such as social learning theory, social cognitive theory, alcohol expectancy theory, problem behavior theory, social identity theory, the theory of reasoned action, the theory of planned behavior, and prototype willingness model as compared to social comparison theory, self-derogation theory, deviance regulation theory, peer cluster theory, and reactance theory. While having weaker explanatory, predictive, or generative power may be associated with when the theory was developed or how broad the theory is, future experimental and longitudinal research is needed for these latter theories to solidify their application to alcohol use among adolescents and young adults.

An additional criterion for a good psychological theory is its value at addressing the conditions that necessitated the creation of the theory – i.e., prevention of alcohol use in adolescents and young adults. As indicated above, it appears as if many of these theories have empirical support related to the etiology of alcohol use in adolescents and young adults. However, reviewing this literature highlights that many of these theories have not been evaluated in the context of prevention of alcohol use in adolescents and young adults, such as social comparison theory, self-derogation theory, deviance regulation theory, and reactance theory. As such, future research is needed to apply these theories of social influence by testing the efficacy of theoretically-based preventative interventions aimed to reduce alcohol use among adolescents and young adults.

Although each of these theories of social influence is distinct, many of these theories have similarities or overlapping components, such as the theory of reasoned action and the prototype/willingness model. Thus, additional research is needed to test competing theories of social influence when applied to etiology and prevention of adolescent and young adult alcohol use. Related, we can have greater confidence in conclusions that are derived from different sources. Common factors arising from multiple theories of social influence as related to alcohol include the importance of peers, family environment and socialization (i.e., risk and protective factors), social norms, and behavior as a means of distinguishing one's self or one's group. It seems clear that each of these factors plays an important role in influencing the drinking of adolescents and young adults. However, more research is needed to consider their mutual and interactive influences across perspectives and to consider how these factors might be used in combination in the development of alcohol interventions.

Alcohol use among adolescents and young adults continues to be problematic, thus creating a need for etiology and prevention research. Many of the theories presented in this book are useful in terms of understanding why adolescents and young adults initiate and engage in alcohol use as well as considering how to best reduce the incidence of alcohol use among these populations.

AUTHOR NOTE

Manuscript preparation was supported by National Institute on Alcohol Abuse and Alcoholism Grants K01AA016966 (awarded to M. A. Lewis), R01AA014576 (awarded to C. Neighbors), and K99AA017669 (awarded to K. P. Lindgren).

REFERENCES

Abbey, A., Zawacki, T., Buck, P. O., Clinton, A. M., and McAuslan, P. (2004). Sexual assault and alcohol consumption: What do we know about their relationship and what types of research are still needed? *Aggression and Violent Behavior, 9,* 271-303.

Abrams, D. B., and Niaura, R. S. (1987). Social learning theory. In Blane, H. T. and Leonard, K. E. (Eds.), *Psychological Theories of Drinking and Alcoholism* (pp. 131-178). New York: Guildford.

Ajzen, I. (1988). *Attitudes, personality, and behavior.* Chicago: Dorsey Press.

Ajzen, I. (1991). The theory of planned behavior. *Organizational Behavior and Human Decision Processes, 50,* 179-211.

Ajzen, I., and Fishbein, M. (1980). *Understanding attitudes and predicting social behavior.*Englewood Cliffs, NJ: Prentice Hall.

Allen, D., Sprenkel, D., and Vitale, P. (1994). Reactance theory and alcohol consumption laws: Further confirmation among collegiate alcohol consumers. *Journal of Studies on Alcohol, 55,* 34-40.

Andrews, J. (1995). The effectiveness of alcohol warning labels: A review and extension. *American Behavioral Scientist, 38,* 622-632.

Andrews, J. A., Hampson, S. E., Barckley, M., Gerrard, M., and Gibbons, F. X. (2008). The effect of early cognitions on cigarette and alcohol use during adolescence. *Psychology of Addictive Behaviors, 22,* 96-106.

Andrews, J. A., Hops, H., and Duncan, S. C. (1997). Adolescent modeling of parent substance use: The moderating effect of the relationship with the parent. *Journal of Family Psychology, 11,* 259-270.

Andrews, J. A., Tildesley, E., Hops, H., and Li, F. (2002). The influence of peers on young adult substance use. *Health Psychology, 21,* 349-357.

Armitage, C. J., and Conner, M. (2001). Efficacy of the theory of planned behaviour: A meta-analytic review. *British Journal of Social Psychology, 40,* 471-499.

Arnett, J. J. (2000). Emerging adulthood: A theory of development from the late teens through the twenties. *American Psychologist, 55,* 469-480.

Bachman, J. G., Wadsworth, K. N., O'Malley, P. M., Johnston, L. D., and Schulenberg, J. (1997). *Smoking, drinking, and during use in young adulthood: The impacts of new freedoms and new responsibilities.* Mahwah, NJ: Lawrence Erlbaum Associates.

Baer, J. S. (2002). Student factors: Understanding individual variation in college drinking. *Journal of Studies on Alcohol, 14* (Suppl. 14), 40-53.

Baer, J. S., MacClean, M. G., and Marlatt, G. A. (1998). Linking etiology and treatment for adolescent substance use: Toward a better match. In R. Jessor (Ed.), *New perspectives on adolescent risk behavior* (pp.182-220). New York, NY US: Cambridge University Press.

Bandura, A. (1969). *Principles of behavior modification.* New York: Holt, Rinehart, and Winston.

Bandura, A. (1977). *Social learning theory.* Englewood Cliffs, NJ: Prentice Hall.

Bandura A. (1986). *Social foundations of thought and action: A social cognitive theory.* Englewood Cliffs, NJ: Prentice Hall.

Basen-Engquist, K., Edmundson, E., and Parcel, G. (1996). Structure of health risk behavior among high school students. *Journal of Consulting and Clinical Psychology, 64,* 764-775.

Beutler, L. E., Mohr, D. C., Grawe, K., Engle, D., and MacDonald, R. (1991). Looking for differential treatment effects: Cross-cultural predictors of differential psychotherapy efficacy. *Journal of Psychotherapy Integration, 1,* 121-141.

Bingham, C. R., Shope, J. T., and Tang, X. (2005). Drinking behavior from high school to young adulthood: Differences by college education. *Alcoholism: Clinical and Experimental Research, 29,* 2170-2180.

Blanton, H., and Burkley, M. (2008). Deviance regulation theory: Applications to adolescent social influence. In M. J. Prinstein and K. A. Dodge (Eds.), *Understanding peer influence in children and adolescents* (pp. 94-121). New York, NY US: Guilford Press.

Blanton, H. and Christie, C. (2003). Deviance regulation: A theory of action and identity. *Review of General Psychology, 7,* 115-149.

Blanton, H., Gibbons, F. X., Gerrard, M., Conger, K. J., and Smith, G. E. (1997). Role of family and peers in the development of prototypes associated with substance use. *Journal of Family Psychology, 11,* 271-288.

Blanton, H., Koblitz, A., and McCaul, K. D. (2008). Misperceptions about norm misperceptions: Descriptive, injunctive, and affective 'social norming' efforts to change health behaviors. *Social and Personality Psychology Compass, 2/3,* 1379-1399.

Blanton, H., Stuart, A. E., and VandenEijnden, R. J. J. M. (2001). An introduction to deviance-regulation theory: The effect of behavioral norms on message framing. *Personality and Social Psychology Bulletin, 27,* 848-858.

Blume, A., Schmaling, K., and Marlatt, A. (2003). Predictors of change in binge drinking over a 3-month period. *Addictive Behaviors, 28,* 1007-1012.

Borsari, B., and Carey, K. B. (2001). Peer influences on college drinking: A review of the research. *Journal of Substance Abuse, 13,* 391-424.

Botvin, G. J. (2000). Preventing drug abuse in schools: Social and competence enhancement approaches targeting individual-level etiologic factors. *Addictive Behaviors, 25,* 887-897.

Bray, J. H., Adams, G. J., Getz, J. G., and Baer, P.E. (2001). Developmental, family, and ethnic influences on adolescent alcohol usage: A growth curve approach. *Journal of Family Psychology, 15,* 301-314.

Bray, J. H., Adams, G. J., Getz, J. G., and McQueen, A. (2003). Individuation, peers, and adolescent alcohol use: A latent growth analysis. *Journal of Consulting and Clinical Psychology, 71,* 553-564.

Brehm, J. W. (1966). *A theory of psychological reactance.* San Diego, CA: Academic Press.

Brown, S. A., and Tapert, S. F. (2004). Adolescence and the trajectory of alcohol use: Basic to clinical studies. *Annals New York Academy of Sciences, 1021,* 234-244.

Buchmann, A. F., Schmid, B., Blomeyer, D., Becker, K., Treutlein, J., Zimmermann, U. S., et al. (2009). Impact of age of first drink on vulnerability to alcohol-related problems: Testing the marker hypothesis in a prospective study of young adults. *Journal of Psychiatric Research, 15,* 1205-1212.

Buunk, B. P., Collins, R. L., Taylor, S. E., Van Yperen, N. W., and Dakof, G. A. (1990). The affective consequences of social-comparison - either direction has its ups and downs. *Journal of Personality and Social Psychology, 59,* 1238-1249.

Buunk, B. P., and Gibbons, F. X. (1997). *Health, coping, and well-being: Perspectives from social comparison theory.* Mahwah, NJ US: Lawrence Erlbaum Associates Publishers.

Cameron, K. A., and Campo, S. (2006). Stepping back from social norms campaigns: Comparing normative influences to other predictors of health behaviors. *Health Communication, 20,* 277-288.

Campo, S., and Cameron, K. A. (2006). Differential effects of exposure to social norms campaigns: A cause for concern. *Health Communication, 19,* 209-219.

Carey, K. B. (1995). Alcohol-related expectancies predict quantity and frequency of heavy drinking among college students. *Psychology of Addictive Behaviors, 9,* 236–241.

Carey, K. B., Borsari, B., Carey, M. P., and Maisto, S. A. (2006). Patterns and importance of self-other differences in college drinking norms. *Psychology of Addictive Behaviors, 20,* 385-393.

Carey, K. B., Scott-Sheldon, L. A. J., Carey, M. P., and DeMartini, K. S. (2007). Individual-level interventions to reduce college student drinking: A meta-analytic review. *Addictive Behaviors, 32,* 2469-2494.

Casswell, S., Pledger, M., and Pratap, S. (2002). Trajectories of drinking from 18 to 26 years: Identification and prediction. *Addiction, 97,* 1427-1437.

Christensen, P. N., Rothgerber, H., Wood, W., and Matz, D. C. (2004). Social norms and identity relevance: A motivational approach to normative behavior. *Personality and Social Psychology Bulletin, 30,* 1295-1309.

Clapp, J. D., Lange, J. E., Russell, C., Shillington, A., and Voas, R. B. (2003). A failed norms social marketing campaign. *Journal of Studies on Alcohol, 64,* 409-414.

Clapper, R., Buka, S., Goldfield, E., and Lipsitt, L. (1995). Adolescent problem behaviors as predictors of adult alcohol diagnoses. *International Journal of the Addictions, 30,* 507-523.

Collins, R. L. (1996). For better or worse: The impact of upward social comparison on self-evaluations. *Psychological Bulletin, 119,* 51-69.

Collins, S. E., and Carey, K. B. (2007). The theory of planned behavior as a model of heavy episodic drinking among college students. *Psychology of Addictive Behaviors, 21,* 498-507.

Conner, M., and Armitage, C. J. (1998). Extending the theory of planned behavior: A review and avenues for further research. *Journal of Applied Social Psychology, 28,* 1429–1464.

Conner, M., Warren, R., Close, S., and Sparks, P. (1999). Alcohol consumption and the theory of planned behavior: An examination of the cognitive mediation of past behavior. *Journal of Applied Social Psychology, 29*, 1676-1704.

Costa, F. M., Jessor, R., and Turbin, M. S. (1999). Transition into adolescent problem drinking: The role of psychosocial risk and protective factors. *Journal of Studies on Alcohol, 60*, 480-490.

Courtney, K. E., and Polich, J. (2009). Binge drinking in young adults: Data, definitions, and determinants. *Psychological Bulletin, 135*, 142-156.

Curran, P. J., Stice, E., and Chassin, L. (1997). The relation between adolescent alcohol use and peer alcohol use: A longitudinal random coefficients model. *Journal of Consulting and Clinical Psychology, 65*, 130-140.

DeCourville, N. H. (1995). Testing the applicability of problem behavior theory to substance use in a longitudinal study. *Psychology of Addictive Behaviors, 9*, 53-66.

DeJong, W., Schneider, S. K., Towvim, L. G., Murphy, M. J., Doerr, E. E., Simonsen, N. R., et al. (2006). A multisite randomized trial of social norms marketing campaigns to reduce college student drinking. *Journal of Studies on Alcohol, 67*, 868-879.

Del Boca, F. K., and Darkes, J. (2001) Is the glass half full or half empty? An evaluation of the status of expectancies as causal agents. *Addiction, 96*, 1681-1683

Dillard, J., and Shen, L. (2005). On the nature of reactance and its role in persuasive health communication. *Communication Monographs, 72*, 144-168.

Dishion, T. J., McCord, J., and Poulin, F. (1999). When interventions harm: Peer groups and problem behavior. *American Psychologist, 54*, 755–764.

Donovan, J. E., and Jessor, R. (1985). Structure of problem behavior in adolescence and young adulthood. *Journal of Consulting and Clinical Psychology, 53*, 890-904.

Donovan, J., Jessor, R., and Costa, F. (1999). Adolescent problem drinking: Stability of psychosocial and behavioral correlates across a generation. *Journal of Studies on Alcohol, 60*, 352-361.

Duncan, S. C., Duncan, T. E., and Strycker, L. A. (2006). Alcohol use from ages 9 to 16: A cohort-sequential latent growth model. *Drug and Alcohol Dependence, 81*, 71-81.

Dunn, M. E., and Goldman, M. S. (1998). Age and drinking-related differences in the memory organization of alcohol expectances in 3rd-, 6th-, 9th-, and 12th-grade children. *Journal of Consulting and Clinical Psychology, 66*, 579–585.

Engels, R. C. M. E., Hermans, R., Baaren, R. B., Hollenstein, T., and Bot, S. M. (2009). Alcohol portrayal on television affects actual drinking behaviour. *Alcohol and Alcoholism, 44*, 244-249.

Engs, R., and Hanson, D. (1989). Reactance theory: A test with collegiate drinking. *Psychological Reports, 64*, 1083-1086.

Epstein, J. A., Zhou, X. K., Bang, H., and Botvin, G. (2007). Do competence skills moderate the impact of social influences to drink and perceived social benefits of drinking on alcohol use among inner-city adolescents? *Prevention Science, 8,* 65-73.

Farrell, A., Danish, S., and Howard, C. (1992). Relationship between drug use and other problem behaviors in urban adolescents. *Journal of Consulting and Clinical Psychology, 60,* 705-712.

Festinger, L. (1954). A theory of social comparison processes. *Human Relations, 7,* 117-140.

Fishbein, M., and Ajzen, I. *(1975). Belief, attitude, intention, and behavior: An introduction totheory and research.* Reading, MA: Addison-Wesley.

Fromme, K., Stroot, E., and Kaplan, D. (1993). Comprehensive effects of alcohol: Development and psychometric assessment of a new expectancy questionnaire. *Psychological Assessment, 5*, 19-26.

Gerrard, M., Gibbons, F. X., Brody, G. H., McBride Murry, V., Cleveland, M. J., and Wills, T. A. (2006). A theory-based dual-focus alcohol intervention for preadolescents: The strong African American families program. *Psychology of Addictive Behaviors, 20*, 185-195.

Gerrard, M., Gibbons, F. X., Houlihan, A. E., Stock, M. L., and Pomery, E. A. (2008). A dual-process approach to health risk decision making: The prototype willingness model. *Developmental Review, 28,* 29-61.

Gerrard, M., Gibbons, F. X., Reis-Bergan, M., Trudeau, L., Vande Lune, L. S., and Buunk, B. (2002). Inhibitory effects of drinker and nondrinker prototypes on adolescent alcohol consumption. *Health Psychology, 21,* 601-609.

Gibbons, F. X., Gerrard, M., Blanton, H., and Russell, D. W. (1998). Reasoned action and social reaction: Willingness and intention as independent predictors of health risk. *Journal of Personality and Social Psychology, 74,* 1164-1180.

Gibbons, F. X., Gerrard, M., Lane, D. J., Mahler, H. I. M., and Kulik, J. A. (2005). Using UV photography to reduce use of tanning booths: A test of cognitive mediation. *Health Psychology, 24,* 358–363.

Gilles, D. M., Turk, C. L., and Fresco, D. M. (2006). Social anxiety, alcohol expectancies, and self-efficacy as predictors of heavy drinking in college students. *Addictive Behaviors, 31*, 388-398.

Gillmore, M. R., Hawkins, J. D., Catalano, R. F., Day, L. E., Moore, M., and Abbott, R. (1991). Structure of problem behaviors in preadolescence. *Journal of Consulting and Clinical Psychology, 59*, 499–506.

Goldman, M. S., Del Boca, F., and Darkes, J. (1999). Alcohol expectancy theory. In K. E. Leonard and H. T. Blane (Eds.), *Psychological Theories of Drinking and Alcoholism (2nd ed.)* (pp. 203-246). New York: Guilford.

Gordon, R., and Minor, S. (1992). Attitudes toward a change in the legal drinking age: Reactance versus compliance. *Journal of College Student Development, 33*, 171-176.

Grant, B. F., and Dawson, D. A. (1997). Age at onset of alcohol use and its association with DSM-IV alcohol abuse and dependence: Results from the National Longitudinal Alcohol Epidemiologic Survey. *Journal of Substance Abuse, 9*, 103-110.

Grant, J. D., Scherrer, J. F., Lynskey, M. T., Lyons, M. J., Eisen, S. A., Tsuang, M. T., et al. (2006). Adolescent alcohol use is a risk factor for adult alcohol and drug dependence: Evidence from a twin design. *Psychological Medicine, 36*, 109-118.

Ham, L., and Hope, D. (2003). College students and problematic drinking: A review of the literature. *Clinical Psychology Review, 23*, 719-759.

Hatzenbuehler, M., Corbin, W., and Fromme, K. (2008). Trajectories and determinants of alcohol use among LGB young adults and their heterosexual peers: Results from a prospective study. *Developmental Psychology, 44*, 81-90.

Hawkins, J. D., Catalano, R. F., and Miller, J. Y. (1992). Risk and protective factors for alcohol and other drug problems in adolescence and early adulthood: Implications for substance-abuse prevention. *Psychological Bulletin, 112*, 64-105.

Hays, R. D., Stacy, A. W., and DiMatteo, M. R. (1987). Problem behavior theory and adolescent alcohol use. *Addictive Behaviors, 12*, 189-193.

Helgeson, V. S., and Mickelson, K. D. (1995). Motives for social comparison. *Personality and Social Psychology Bulletin, 21*, 1200-1209.

Heron, M. P. (2007). *Death: Leading causes for 2004.* National Vital Statistics Reports, 56, 1-96. Hyattsville, MD: National Center for Health Statistics.

Hingson, R. W., Heeren, T., and Winter, M. R. (2006). Age at drinking onset and alcohol dependence. *Archives of Pediatrics and Adolescent Medicine, 160*, 739-746.

Hingson, R., Heeren, T., Winter, M., and Wechsler, H. (2005). Magnitude of alcohol-related mortality and morbidity among U.S. college students ages 18-24: Changes from 1998 to 2001. *Annual Review of Public Health, 26,* 259-279.

Hingson, R. W., Heeren, T., Zakocs, R. C., Kopstein, A., and Wechsler, H. (2002). Magnitude of alcohol-related mortality and morbidity among U.S. college students ages 18-24. *Journal of Studies on Alcohol, 63,* 136-144.

Huchting, K., Lac, A., and LaBrie, J. W. (2008). An application of the theory of planned behavior to sorority alcohol consumption. *Addictive Behaviors, 33,* 538-551.

Jessor, R. (1987). Problem-behavior theory, psychosocial development, and adolescent problem drinking. *British Journal of Addiction, 82,* 331-342.

Jessor, R. (1991). Risk behavior in adolescence: A psychosocial framework for understanding and action. *Journal of Adolescent Health, 12,* 597-605.

Jessor, R. (1998). *New perspectives on adolescent risk behavior.* New York, NY US: Cambridge University Press.

Jessor, R., Costa, F., Krueger, P., and Turbin, M. (2006). A developmental study of heavy episodic drinking among college students: The role of psychosocial and behavioral protective and risk factors. *Journal of Studies on Alcohol, 67,* 86-94.

Jessor, R., Donovan, J. E., and Costa, F. M. (1991). *Beyond adolescence: Problem behavior and young adult development.* New York: Cambridge University Press.

Jessor, R., Graves, T. D., Hanson, R. C., and Jessor, S. L. (1968). *Society, personality, and deviant behavior: A study of a tri-ethnic community.* New York: Holt, Rinehart and Winston.

Jessor, R., and Jessor, S. L. (1977). *Problem behavior and psychosocial development: A longitudinal study of youth.* New York: Academic Press.

Jessor, R., Turbin, M. S., Costa, F. M., Dong, Q., Zhang, H., and Wang, C. (2003). Adolescent problem behavior in China and the United States: A cross-national study of psychosocial protective factors. *Journal of Research on Adolescence, 13,* 329–360.

Jessor, R., Van Den Bos, J., Vanderryn, J., Costa, F. M., and Turbin, M. S. (1995). Protective factors in adolescent problem behavior: Moderator effects and developmental change. *Developmental Psychology, 31,* 923-933.

Johnston, L. D., O'Malley, P. M., Bachman, J. G., and Schulenberg, J. E. (2008). *Monitoring the Future national survey results on drug use, 1975–2007: Volume II, College students and adults ages 19–45* (NIH

Publication No. 08-6418B). Bethesda, MD: National Institute on Drug Abuse.

Johnston, L. D., O'Malley, P. M., Bachman, J. G., and Schulenberg, J. E. (2009). *Monitoring the Future national results on adolescent drug use: Overview of key findings, 2008* (NIH Publication No. 09-7401). Bethesda, MD: National Institute on Drug Abuse.

Johnston, K. L., and White, K. M. (2003). Binge-drinking: A test of the role of group norms in the theory of planned behaviour. *Psychology and Health, 18*, 63-77.

Jones, B., Corbin, W., and Fromme, K. (2001). Half full or half empty, the glass still does not satisfactorily quench the thirst for knowledge on alcohol expectancies as a mechanism of change. *Addiction, 96*, 1672-1674.

Jones, E. E., and Davis, K. E. (1965). From acts to dispositions: The attribution process in person perception. In L. Berkowitz (Ed.), *Advance in experimental social psychology* (pp. 220-266). New York: Academic Press.

Kam, J. A., Matsunaga, M., Hecht, M. L., and Ndiaye, K. (2009). Extending the theory of planned behavior to predict alcohol, tobacco, and marijuana use among youth of Mexican heritage. *Prevention Science, 10*, 41-53.

Kaplan, H. B. and Johnson, R. J. (2001). *Social deviance: Testing a general theory*. New York: Kluwer/Plenum.

Kaplan, H. B., Johnson, R. J., and Bailey, C. A. (1987). Deviant peers and deviant behavior: Further elaboration of a model. *Social Psychology Quarterly*, 50, 277-284.

Kaplan, H. B., Martin, S. S., and Robbins, C. (1982). Application of a general theory of deviant behavior: Self-derogation and adolescent drug use. *Journal of Health and Social Behavior, 23*, 274-294.

Kelley, H. H. (1967). Attribution theory in social psychology. *Nebraska Symposium on Motivation, 15,* 192-238.

Kidorf, M., Sherman, M. F., Johnson, J. G., and Bigelow, G. E. (1995). Alcohol expectancies and changes in beer consumption of first-year college students. *Addictive Behaviors, 20,* 225–231.

Kuther, T. L., and Higgins-D'Alessandro, A. (2003). Attitudinal and normative predictors of alcohol use by older adolescents and young adults. *Journal of Drug Education, 33,* 71-90.

Larimer, M. E., and Cronce, J. M. (2002). Identification, prevention, and treatment: A review of individual-focused strategies to reduce problematic alcohol consumption by college students. *Journal of Studies on Alcohol, 14,* 148-163.

Larimer, M. E., and Cronce, J. M. (2007). Identification, prevention, and treatment revisited: Individual-focused college drinking prevention strategies 1999-2006. *Addictive Behaviors, 32,* 2439-2468.

Larimer, M. E., Kaysen, D. L., Lee, C. M., Kilmer, J. R., Lewis, M. A., Dillworth, T., Montoya, H., and Neighbors, C. (2009). Evaluating levels of specificity in normative referents in relation to personal drinking behavior. *Journal of Studies on Alcohol and Drugs, s16,* 115-121.

Larimer, M. E., Lee, C. M., Kilmer, J. R., Fabiano, P. M., Stark, C. B., Geisner, I. M., et al. (2007). Personalized mailed feedback for college drinking prevention: A randomized clinical trial. *Journal of Consulting and Clinical Psychology, 75,* 285-293.

Larsen, H., Engels, R., Granic, I., and Overbeek, G. (2009). An experimental study on imitation of alcohol consumption in same-sex dyads. *Alcohol and Alcoholism, 44,* 250-255.

Latendresse, S. J., Rose, R. J., Viken, R. J., Pulkkinen, L., Kaprio, J., and Dick, D. M. (2008). Parenting mechanisms in links between parents' and adolescents' alcohol use behaviors. *Alcoholism: Clinical and Experimental Research, 32,* 322-330.

Leary, M. R., Tambor, E. S., Terdal, S. K., and Downs, D. L. (1995). Self-esteem as an interpersonal monitor - the Sociometer Hypothesis. *Journal of Personality and Social Psychology, 68,* 518-530.

Lewis, M. A. and Neighbors, C. (2004). Gender-specific misperceptions of college student drinking norms. *Psychology of Addictive Behaviors, 18,* 334-339.

Lewis, M. A. and Neighbors, C. (2007). Optimizing personalized normative feedback: The use of gender-specific referents. *Journal of Studies on Alcohol and Drugs, 68,* 228-237.

Lewis, M. A., Neighbors, C., Oster-Aaland, L., Kirkeby, B. S., and Larimer, M. E. (2007). Indicated prevention for incoming freshmen: Personalized feedback and high-risk drinking. *Addictive Behaviors, 32,* 2495-2508.

Lewis, M. A., Phillippi, J., and Neighbors, C. (2007). Morally based self-esteem, drinking motives, and alcohol use among college students. *Psychology of Addictive Behaviors, 21,* 398-403.

Luhtanen, R. K., and Crocker, J. (2005). Alcohol use in college students: Effects of level of self-esteem, narcissism, and contingencies of self-worth. *Psychology of Addictive Behaviors, 19,* 99-103.

MacAndrew, C., and Edgerton, R. B. (1969). *Drunken comportment: A social explanation*. Oxford, England: Aldine.

MacCorquodale, K., and Meehl, P. E. (1953). Preliminary suggestions as to a formalization of expectancy theory. *Psychological Review, 60*, 55-63.

MacKinnon, D. P., Nohre, L., Cheong, J., and Stacy, A. W. (2001). Longitudinal relationship between the alcohol warning label and alcohol consumption. *Journal Studies on Alcohol, 62,* 221-227.

Maisto, S., Carey, K., and Bradizza, C. (1999). Social learning theory. *Psychological theories of drinking and alcoholism (2nd ed.)* (pp. 106-163). New York: Guilford Press.

Marcoux, B. C. and Shope, J. T. (1997). Application of the theory of planned behavior to adolescent use and misuse of alcohol. *Health Education Research, 12,* 323-331.

Marlatt, G. A. and Donovan, D. M. (2005). *Relapse prevention: Maintenance strategies in the treatment of addictive behaviors (2nd ed.)*. New York: Guilford Press.

Martino, S., Collins, R., Ellickson, P., Schell, T., and McCaffrey, D. (2006). Socio-environmental influences on adolescents' alcohol outcome expectancies: A prospective analysis. *Addiction, 101,* 971-983.

Mason, W. A. (2001). Self-esteem and delinquency revisited (again): A test of Kaplan's self-derogation theory of delinquency using latent growth curve modeling. *Journal of Youth and Adolescence, 30,* 83-102.

Mattern, J. L. and Neighbors, C. (2004). Social norms campaigns: examining the relationship between changes in perceived norms and changes in drinking levels. *Journal of Studies on Alcohol, 65,* 489-493.

McCarthy, D., Aarons, G., and Brown, S. (2002). Educational and occupational attainment and drinking behavior: An expectancy model in young adulthood. *Addiction, 97,* 717-726.

McMillan, B., and Conner, M. (2003). Using the theory of planned behaviour to understand alcohol and tobacco use in students. *Psychology, Health and Medicine, 8,* 317-328.

Miller, C. H., Lane, L. T., Deatrick, L. M., Young, A. M., and Potts, K. A. (2007). Psychological reactance and promotional health messages: The effects of controlling language, lexical concreteness, and the restoration of freedom. *Health Communication Research, 33,* 219-240.

Miller, P. M., Smith, G. T., and Goldman, M. S. (1990). Emergence of alcohol expectancies in childhood: A possible critical period. *Journal of Studies on Alcohol, 51,* 343–349.

Miller, W. R., and Rollnick, S. (1991). *Motivational interviewing: Preparing people to change addictive behavior.* New York: Guilford.

Miller, W. R., and Rollnick, S. (2002). *Motivational interviewing: Preparing people for* change (2nd ed.). New York: Guilford.

Mitchell, C. M., Beals, J., and Kaufman, C. E. (2006). Alcohol use, outcome expectancies, and HIV risk status among American Indian youth: A latent growth curve model with parallel processes. *Journal of Youth and Adolescence, 35,* 729-740.

Neighbors, C., LaBrie, J. W., Hummer, J. F., Lewis, M. A., Lee, C. M., Desai, S., et al. (2009). Group identification as a moderator of the relationship between social norms and alcohol consumption. Manuscript submitted for publication.

Neighbors, C., Larimer, M. E., and Lewis, M. A. (2004). Targeting misperceptions of descriptive drinking norms: Efficacy of a computer delivered personalized normative feedback intervention. *Journal of Consulting and Clinical Psychology, 72,* 434-447.

Neighbors, C., Lee, C. M., Lewis, M. A., Fossos, N., and Larimer, M. E. (2007). Are social norms the best predictor of outcomes among heavy-drinking college students? *Journal of Studies on Alcohol and Drugs, 68,* 556-565.

Neighbors, C., Lewis, M. A., Bergstrom, R. L., and Larimer, M. E. (2006). Being controlled by normative influences: Self-determination as a moderator of a normative feedback alcohol intervention. *Health Psychology, 25,* 571-579.

Neighbors, C., Palmer, R. S., and Larimer, M. E. (2004). Interest and participation in a college student alcohol intervention study as a function of typical drinking. *Journal of Studies on Alcohol, 65,* 736-740.

Norman, P., Armitage, C. J., and Quigley, C. (2007). The theory of planned behavior and binge drinking: Assessing the impact of binge drinker prototypes. *Addictive Behaviors, 32,* 1753-1768.

Norman, P., and Conner, M. (2006). The theory of planned behaviour and binge drinking: Assessing the moderating role of past behaviour within the theory of planned behaviour. *British Journal of Health Psychology, 11,* 55-70.

O'Callaghan, F. V., Chant, D. C., Callan, V. J., and Baglioni, A. (1996). Models of alcohol use by young adults: An examination of various attitude–behavior theories. *Journal of Studies on Alcohol, 58,* 502–507.

O'Connor, R. M., Farrow, S., and Colder, C. R. (2008). Clarifying the anxiety sensitivity and alcohol use relation: Considering alcohol expectancies as moderators. *Journal of Studies on Alcohol and Drugs, 69,* 765-772.

O'Malley, P. M., and Johnston, L. D. (2002). Epidemiology of alcohol and other drug use among American college students. *Journal of Studies on Alcohol, 14,* 23-39.

Oetting, E. R., and Beauvais, F. (1986). Peer cluster theory: Drugs and the adolescent. *Journal of Counseling and Development, 65,* 17-22.

Oetting, E. R., and Beauvais, F. (1987). Peer cluster theory, socialization characteristics, and adolescent drug use: A path analysis. *Journal of Counseling Psychology, 34,* 205-213.

Oetting, E. R., and Lynch, R. S. (2006). Peers and the prevention of adolescent drug use. In Z. Sloboda and W. J. Bukoski (Eds.), *Handbook of drug abuse prevention: Theory, science, and practice* (pp.101-127). New York, NY: Springer.

Ouellette, J. A., and Wood, W. (1998). Habit and intention in everyday life: The multiple processes by which past behavior predicts future behavior. *Psychological Bulletin, 124,* 54-74.

Perkins, H., and Berkowitz, A. (1989). Stability and contradiction in college students' drinking following a drinking-age law change. *Journal of Alcohol and Drug Education, 35,* 60-77.

Perkins, H. W., and Craig, D. W. (2006). A successful social norms campaign to reduce alcohol misuse among college student-athletes. *Journal of Studies on Alcohol, 67,* 880-889.

Petraitis, J., Flay, B. R., and Miller, T. Q. (1995). Reviewing theories of adolescent substance use: Organizing pieces in the puzzle. *Psychological Bulletin, 117,* 67-86.

Perkins, H. W., Haines, M. P., and Rice, R. (2005). Misperceiving the college drinking norm and related problems: A nationwide study of exposure to prevention information, perceived norms and student alcohol misuse. *Journal of Studies on Alcohol, 66,* 470-478.

Quigley, B. M., and Collins, R. L. (1999). The modeling of alcohol consumption: A meta-analytic review. *Journal of Studies of Alcohol, 60,* 90-98.

Radin, S. M., Neighbors, C., Walker, P. S., Walker, R. D., Marlatt, G. A., and Larimer, M. E. (2006). The changing influences of self-worth and peer deviance on drinking problems in urban American Indian adolescents. *Psychology of Addictive Behaviors, 20,* 161-170.

Rains, S. A., and Turner, M. M. (2007). Psychological reactance and persuasive health communication: A test and extension of the intertwined model. *Health Communication Research, 33,* 241-269.

Read, J. P., Wood, M. D., and Capone, C. (2005). A prospective investigation of relations between social influences and alcohol involvement during the transition into college. *Journal of Studies on Alcohol, 66,* 23-34.

Reed, M. B., Lange, J. E., Ketchie, J. M., and Clapp, J. D. (2007). The relationship between social identity, normative information, and college student drinking. *Social Influence, 2,* 269-294.

Ricciardelli, L., and McCabe, M. (2008). University students' perceptions of the alcohol campaign: "Is getting pissed getting pathetic? (Just ask your friends)". *Addictive Behaviors, 33,* 366-372.

Rivis, A., Sheeran, P., and Armitage, C. J. (2006). Augmenting the theory of planned behaviour with the prototype/willingness model: Predictive validity of actor versus abstainer prototypes for adolescents' health-protective and health-risk intentions. *British Journal of Health Psychology, 11,* 483-500.

Rotter, J. (1954). *Social learning and clinical psychology.* Englewood Cliffs, NJ: Prentice-Hall, Inc.

Substance Abuse and Mental Health Services Administration. (2008). *Results from the 2007 National Survey on Drug Use and Health: National findings.* Office of Applied Studies. Rockville, MD.

Schell, T., Martino, S., Ellickson, P., Collins, R., and McCaffrey, D. (2005). Measuring developmental changes in alcohol expectancies. *Psychology of Addictive Behaviors, 19,* 217-220.

Schinke, S. P., Cole, K. C. A., and Fang, L. (2009). Gender-specific intervention to reduce underage drinking among early adolescent girls: A test of a computer-mediated, mother-daughter program. *Journal of Studies on Alcohol and Drugs, 70,* 70-77.

Schlegel, R. P., D'Avernas, J. R., Zanna, M. P., DeCourville, N. H., and Manske, S. R. (1992). Problem drinking: A problem for the theory of reasoned action? *Journal of Applied Social Psychology, 22,* 358–385.

Schroeder, C. M., and Prentice, D. A. (1998). Exposing pluralistic ignorance to reduce alcohol use among college students. *Journal of Applied Social Psychology, 28,* 2150-2180.

Schulenberg, J. E., and Maggs, J. L. (2002). A developmental perspective on alcohol use and heavy drinking during adolescence and the transition to young adulthood. *Journal of Studies on Alcohol, 14,* 54-70.

Sher, K. J., Wood, M. D., Wood, P. K., and Raskin, G. (1996). Alcohol outcome expectancies and alcohol use: A latent variable cross-lagged panel study. *Journal of Abnormal Psychology, 105,* 561-574.

Shoham, V., Trost, S., and Rohrbaugh, M. (2004). From state to trait and back again: Reactance theory goes clinical. *Motivational analyses of social behavior: Building on Jack Brehm's contributions to psychology* (pp. 167-185). Mahwah, NJ US: Lawrence Erlbaum Associates Publishers.

Shoham-Salomon, V., and Hannah, M. T. (1991). Client-treatment interaction in the study of differential change processes. *Journal of Consulting and Clinical Psychology, 57,* 590-598.

Slutske, W. (2005). Alcohol use disorders among U.S. college students and their non-college-attending peers. *Archives of General Psychiatry, 62,* 321-327.

Smith, G. T., Goldman, M. S., Greenbaum, P. E., and Christiansen, B. A. (1995). Expectancy of social facilitation from drinking: The divergent paths of high-expectancy and low-expectancy adolescents. *Journal of Abnormal Psychology, 104,* 32-40.

Spijkerman, R., van den Eijnden, R. J. J. M., Vitale, S., and Engels, R. C. M. E. (2004). Explaining adolescents' smoking and drinking behavior: The concept of smoker and drinker prototypes in relation to variables of the theory of planned behavior. *Addictive Behaviors, 29,* 1615-1622.

Squeglia, L. M., Jacobus, J., and Tapert, S. F. (2009). The influence of substance use on adolescent brain development. *Clinical EEG and Neuroscience Journal, 40,* 31-38.

Stapel, D. A., and Blanton, H. (2007). *Social comparison theories: Key readings.* New York: Psychology Press.

Stein, J. A., Newcomb, M. D., and Bentler, P. M. (1987). Personality and drug use: Reciprocal effects across four years. *Personality and Individual Differences, 8,* 419-430.

Stuart, A. E., and Blanton, H. (2003). The effects of message framing on behavioral prevalence assumptions. *European Journal of Social Psychology, 33,* 93-102.

Suls, J., and Green, P. (2003). Pluralistic ignorance and college student perceptions of gender- specific alcohol norms. *Health Psychology, 22,* 479-486.

Suls, J., and Wheeler, L. (2000). *Handbook of social comparison: Theory and research.* (vols.2000) Dordrecht, Netherlands: Kluwer Academic Publishers.

Suls, J., and Wills, T. A. (1991). *Social comparison: Contemporary theory and research*. Hillsdale, NJ England: Lawrence Erlbaum Associates, Inc.

Swaim, R. C., Oetting, E. R., Edwards, R. W., and Beauvais, F. (1989). Links from emotional distress to adolescent drug use: A path model. *Journal of Consulting and Clinical Psychology, 57*, 227-231.

Tajfel, H., and Turner, J. C. (1986). The social identity theory of intergroup behavior. In S. Worchel and W. G. Austin (Eds.), *Psychology of intergroup relations* (pp. 7-24). Chicago: Nelson-Hall.

Tevyaw, T. O., Borsari, B., Colby, S. M., and Monti, P. M. (2007). Peer enhancement of a brief motivational intervention with mandated college students. *Psychology of Addictive Behaviors, 21*, 114-119.

Thombs, D. L., and Hamilton, M. J. (2002). Effects of a social norm feedback campaign on the drinking norms and behavior of Division I student-athletes. *Journal of Drug Education, 32*, 227-244.

Thush, C., and Wiers, R.W. (2007). Explicit and implicit alcohol-related cognitions and the prediction of future drinking in adolescents. *Addictive Behaviors, 32,* 1367-1383.

Tolman, E. (1932). *Purposive behavior in animals and men*. London England: Century/Random House.

Turner, J. C., Hogg, M. A., Oakes, P. J., Reicher, S. D., and Wetherell, M. S. (1987).*Rediscovering the social group: A self-categorization theory*. Oxford, UK: Blackwell.

U.S. Department of Health and Human Services. (2007). *The Surgeon General's Call to Action To Prevent and Reduce Underage Drinking*. Department of Health and Human Services, Office of the Surgeon General. Washington, DC.

Valdivia, I., and Stewart, S.H. (2005). Further examination of the psychometric properties of the comprehensive effects of alcohol questionnaire. *Cognitive Behaviour Therapy, 34*, 22-33.

Wall, A., Hinson, R., McKee, S., and Goldstein, A. (2001). Examining alcohol outcome expectancies in laboratory and naturalistic bar settings: A within-subject experimental analysis. *Psychology of Addictive Behaviors, 15*, 219-226.

Wall, A., McKee, S., and Hinson, R. (2000). Assessing variation in alcohol outcome expectancies across environmental context: An examination of the situational-specificity hypothesis. *Psychology of Addictive Behaviors, 14*, 367-375.

Walter, S. T., and Neighbors, C. (2005). Feedback interventions for college alcohol misuse: What, why and for whom? *Addictive Behaviors, 30,* 1168-1182.

Wechsler, H., Davenport, A., Dowdall, G., Moeykens, B., and Castillo, S. (1994). Health and behavioral consequences of binge drinking in college: A national survey of students at 140 campuses. *Journal of the American Medical Association, 272,* 1672-1677.

Wechsler, H., Lee, J. E., Nelson, T. F., and Lee, H. (2003). Drinking and driving among college students: The influence of alcohol-control policies. *American Journal of Preventive Medicine, 25,* 212-218.

Weiss, B., Caron, A., Ball, S., Tapp, J., Johnson, M., and Weisz, J. R. (2005). Iatrogenic effects of group treatment for antisocial youths. *Journal of Consulting and Clinical Psychology, 73,* 1036–1044.

Werch, C. E., Pappas, D. M., Carlson, J. M., DiClemente, C. C., Chally, P. S., and Sinder, J. A. (2000). Results of a social norm intervention to prevent binge drinking among first-year residential college students. *Journal of American College Health, 49,* 85-92.

Wheeler, L. (1966). Motivation as a determinant of upward comparison. *Journal of Experimental Social Psychology, 2,* 27-31.

White, H. R., McMorris, B. J., Catalano, R. F., Fleming, C. B., Haggerty, K. P., and Abbott, R. D. (2006). Increases in alcohol and marijuana use during the transition out of high school into emerging adulthood: The effects of leaving home, going to college, and high school protective factors. *Journal of Studies on Alcohol, 67,* 810-822.

Willoughby, T., Chalmers, H., and Busseri, M. (2004). Where is the syndrome? Examining co-occurrence among multiple problem behaviors in adolescence. *Journal of Consulting and Clinical Psychology, 72,* 1022-1037.

Wills, T. A. (1981). Downward comparison principles in social psychology. *Psychological Bulletin, 90,* 245-271.

Yanovitzky, I., Stewart, L. P., and Lederman, L. C. (2006). Social distance, perceived drinking by peers, and alcohol use by college students. *Health Communication, 19,* 1-10.

Young, R. M., Connor, J. P., Ricciardelli, L. A., and Saunders, J. B. (2006). The role of alcohol expectancy and drinking refusal self-efficacy beliefs in university student drinking. *Alcohol and Alcoholism, 41,* 70-75.

Young, R. M., Hasking, P. A. Oei, T. P. S., and Loveday, W. (2007). Validation of the drinking refusal self-efficacy questionnaire: Revised in an adolescent sample (DRSEQ-RA). *Addictive Behaviors, 32,* 862-868.

INDEX

A

abstinence, 6
accuracy, 22
acute, vii
adolescence, 1, 2, 12, 17, 29, 30, 57, 61, 63, 64, 70, 73
adolescent behavior, 45
adolescent boys, 30
adolescent problem behavior, 18, 64
adult, vii, 3, 6, 8, 13, 17, 27, 28, 34, 37, 38, 46, 49, 53, 54, 57, 60, 63, 64
adult population, 28
adulthood, 2, 17, 31, 39, 58, 61, 63, 67, 70, 73
adults, vii, 1, 2, 3, 5, 6, 7, 8, 9, 12, 18, 19, 22, 26, 28, 34, 35, 37, 38, 39, 43, 49, 50, 51, 53, 54, 59, 61, 63, 64, 65, 68
advertisements, 12
age, 1, 7, 12, 15, 17, 35, 38, 50, 59, 63, 69
agents, 16, 61
aid, 28
alcohol abuse, 63
alcohol consumption, 6, 8, 11, 12, 17, 23, 26, 27, 28, 39, 46, 50, 52, 57, 62, 64, 66, 67, 68, 69
alcohol dependence, vii, 1, 63
alcohol research, 49
alcohol use, vii, 1, 2, 5, 6, 8, 9, 12, 16, 18, 22, 23, 26, 27, 28, 30, 34, 35, 38, 39, 42, 43, 46, 49, 50, 52, 53, 54, 57, 59, 61, 62, 63, 65, 66, 68, 69, 70, 71, 73
alcoholism, 67
alternative, 13, 29, 51
alternatives, 41
altruism, 21
animals, 72
anxiety, 13, 63, 69
argument, 22
arousal, 49
assault, 2, 57
assessment, 62
assumptions, 37, 71
athletes, 69, 72
attachment, 30
attitudes, 6, 33, 34, 35, 37, 41, 45, 51, 57
attribution, 41, 65
authority, 50

B

back, 60, 71
beer, 65
behavior modification, 58
behavioral intentions, 33, 37
behavioral medicine, 16
beliefs, 6, 7, 33, 45, 73
benefits, 62
beverages, 7, 50
binge drinking, 7, 59, 68, 73

blacks, 18
blood, 6, 28
brain, 1, 71
brain development, 1, 71

C

campaigns, 50, 60, 61, 67
categorization, 25, 26, 27, 28, 72
categorization theory, 25, 72
causal relationship, 7
childhood, 12, 67
children, 12, 58, 61
clients, 49, 52
clinical psychology, 70
clinical trial, 66
cluster theory, vii, 3, 45, 46, 53, 69
clusters, 45
cognitive process, 5, 7, 13
cognitive psychology, 5
cognitive representations, 25, 38
cohesion, 29, 30
cohort, 61
collaboration, 25
college students, 2, 6, 8, 9, 12, 17, 18, 22,
    28, 30, 34, 39, 42, 47, 51, 60, 63, 64, 65,
    66, 68, 69, 70, 71, 72, 73
colleges, 50
commercials, 7
communication, 6, 50, 51, 61, 70
community, 50, 64
competence, 30, 59, 62
compliance, 49, 63
components, 28, 37, 54
computer software, 17
concentration, 6, 28
conceptualizations, 22
concreteness, 67
condom, 38, 42
confidence, 7, 54
conformity, 41
consumers, 57
consumption, 6, 8, 11, 12, 17, 23, 26, 27,
    28, 39, 46, 49, 50, 52, 57, 60, 62, 64, 65,
    66, 67, 68, 69

control, 6, 15, 16, 33, 34, 35, 73
control condition, 6
correlation, 17
correlations, 17, 18
critical period, 12, 67
culture, 3

D

data analysis, 13
decision making, 37, 38, 53, 62
defensiveness, 52
definition, 25
delinquency, 16, 30, 67
demand characteristic, 50
demographics, 26
Department of Health and Human Services,
    2, 72
determinism, 5, 8, 9
developmental change, 64, 70
deviation, 41
differential treatment, 58
downward comparison, 21, 22
drug abuse, 59, 69
drug dependence, 63
drug treatment, 46
drug use, 16, 29, 45, 62, 64, 65, 69, 71, 72
drugs, 45, 50
DSM-IV, 63

E

education, 65, 67, 69, 72
EEG, 71
ego, 21
elaboration, 65
emotional, 8, 46, 72
emotional distress, 46, 72
encoding, 7
engagement, 7, 15, 16
environment, 5, 7, 8, 18
environmental context, 72
environmental factors, 5, 8, 9
environmental influences, 67

estimating, 26
etiologic factor, 59
etiology, 28, 53, 54, 58
exposure, 12, 16, 42, 60, 69
eyes, 15

F

failure, 29
familial, 29
family, 3, 29, 30, 54, 58, 59
family conflict, 30
family environment, 54
family factors, 30
feedback, 9, 27, 28, 66, 68, 72
feelings, 5
females, 18
flu shot, 42
focusing, 23
framing, 59, 71
freedom, 49, 50, 52, 67
freedoms, 49, 58

G

gender, 13, 26, 28, 35, 66, 71
generalizability, 17
generation, 61
genetics, 16
girls, 70
glass, 61, 65
glasses, 7
goals, 46
government, 51
group membership, 25, 28
group processes, 25
groups, 8, 25, 26, 27, 28, 61
growth, 30, 46, 59, 61, 67, 68

H

harm, 61
health, 2, 5, 9, 16, 37, 43, 49, 51, 58, 59, 60,
    61, 62, 67, 70

Health and Human Services, 72
health psychology, 16
heavy drinking, 1, 2, 43, 60, 63, 70
heuristic, 37
heuristic processing, 37
high school, 1, 2, 46, 58, 73
high-risk, 1, 38, 47, 66
hippocampal, 1
HIV, 68
house, 72
human, 5, 33
human behavior, 5, 33
hypothesis, 46, 59, 72

I

iatrogenic, 43
identification, 25, 26, 27, 28, 31, 68
identity, vii, 3, 25, 26, 41, 53, 58, 60, 70, 72
images, 7, 37, 38, 39, 41
imitation, 66
in situ, 37
incentives, 7, 31
incidence, 54
inclusion, 43, 47
inferences, 42
initiation, vii, 1, 2
injuries, vii, 1, 2
innovation, 43, 53
institutions, 50
intentions, 33, 34, 35, 37, 38, 39, 42, 43, 70
interaction, 71
interrelationships, 5, 9
intervention, 9, 14, 18, 23, 27, 28, 31, 38,
    43, 47, 49, 52, 62, 68, 70, 72, 73
intervention strategies, 27, 43, 52
intoxication, 17

L

language, 67
law, 50, 69
laws, 50, 57
learning, 5, 6, 9, 11, 57, 58, 67, 70

LGB, 63
lifetime, 1
likelihood, 6, 7, 16, 29, 52
limitation, 43, 51
limitations, 51
links, 45, 66
longitudinal study, 7, 46, 61, 64
love, 30

M

maintenance, vii, 2, 5, 9, 67
maladaptive, 19
marijuana, 65, 73
marketing, 27, 50, 60, 61
mass media, 12
maturation, 23
measurement, 13, 34
measures, 13
media, 8, 12
mediation, 61, 62
memory, 1, 11, 61
men, 72
messages, 27, 42, 43, 51, 52, 67
meta-analysis, 47
modeling, 6, 7, 9, 57, 67, 69
models, 6, 7, 8, 9, 11, 12, 17, 18, 34, 35, 53
moderators, 13, 17, 69
morbidity, 64
mortality, 64
motivation, 29
motives, 21, 66
multidimensional, 17
multidimensional scaling, 17
multiple factors, 18

N

narcissism, 66
natural, 21, 47
negative consequences, vii, 2, 6, 9, 22, 53
negative reinforcement, 5
neglect, 29, 46
NIH, 64, 65

normative behavior, 26, 27, 60
norms, 15, 17, 22, 26, 27, 28, 29, 33, 34, 35,
    37, 41, 42, 50, 54, 59, 60, 61, 65, 66, 67,
    68, 69, 71, 72

O

objective criteria, 21
occupational, 67
openness, 37

P

parental support, 30
parenting, 39
parents, 3, 6, 7, 12, 66
passive, 9
path analysis, 69
path model, 72
pathways, 39
patients, 49
PBT, 15, 16, 17, 18
peer, vii, 3, 7, 8, 12, 22, 23, 27, 29, 30, 45,
    46, 53, 58, 61, 69
peer group, 8, 27, 45
peer influence, 7, 8, 22, 30, 58
peer rejection, 29
peers, 2, 3, 5, 7, 8, 12, 26, 27, 29, 30, 46, 54,
    57, 58, 59, 63, 65, 71, 73
perceived control, 34
perceived norms, 26, 42, 67, 69
perception, 27, 65
perceptions, 26, 27, 28, 33, 70, 71
personal identity, 41
personality, 15, 18, 57, 64
pharmacological, 12
play, 7, 16
pluralistic, 22, 70
poor, vii, 2, 29, 34
population, 23
positive correlation, 16
power, 53
preadolescents, 62
predictability, 35

prediction, 16, 26, 34, 60, 72
predictive validity, 35
predictors, 13, 22, 34, 35, 58, 60, 62, 63, 65
pressure, 8
prevention, 9, 23, 28, 39, 43, 46, 49, 50, 53, 54, 63, 65, 66, 67, 69
probability, 45
problem behavior, vii, 3, 15, 16, 17, 18, 53, 60, 61, 62, 63, 64, 73
Problem Behavior Theory, v, 15, 30, 31
problem behaviors, 15, 16, 17, 18, 60, 62, 63, 73
problem drinking, 16, 17, 18, 61, 64
program, 62, 70
prosocial behavior, 16
protective factors, 16, 17, 30, 54, 61, 63, 64, 73
prototype, vii, 3, 37, 38, 39, 53, 54, 62, 70
psychology, 71
psychometric properties, 72
psychosocial development, 64
psychosocial factors, 46
psychotherapy, 58
public, 2, 49, 50
public health, 2, 49
punishment, 5, 11

Q

questioning, 50
questionnaire, 62, 72, 73

R

race, 26
random, 61
range, 34
ratings, 47
reactant, 49
reflection, 38
regulation, vii, 3, 7, 41, 53, 54, 58, 59
reinforcement, 5, 6, 11
rejection, 29
relationship, 7, 9, 12, 22, 26, 27, 28, 30, 38, 46, 57, 67, 68, 70

relationships, 8, 26, 35, 46
relaxation, 5
relevance, 60
residential, 73
resistance, 46, 52
resolution, 13
responsibilities, 58
rewards, 6
risk, 1, 5, 9, 16, 17, 23, 28, 30, 31, 37, 38, 47, 54, 58, 61, 62, 63, 64, 66, 68, 70
risk behaviors, 5, 9, 23, 38
risk factors, 16, 17, 28, 30, 31, 64
risks, 2

S

sample, 8, 9, 17, 30, 34, 73
satisfaction, 47
scaling, 17
school, 1, 2, 16, 46, 50, 58, 59, 73
self-concept, 25
self-conception, 25
self-destruction, 21
self-efficacy, 6, 7, 13, 34, 35, 63, 73
self-enhancement, 25
self-esteem, 25, 29, 30, 66
self-evaluations, 60
self-improvement, 21, 22
self-regulation, 7
self-report, 13
self-worth, 29, 30, 41, 66, 69
semantic, 16
sensitivity, 13, 69
sex, 2, 6, 26, 42, 66
sexual activities, vii
sexual activity, 16
sexual assault, 2
sexual behavior, 16
sexual orientation, 13
shape, 8, 45
shares, 31
siblings, 7
skills training, 9, 46
smoking, 38, 71
social behavior, 41, 57, 71
social benefits, 62

social categorization, 25, 26
social category, 25
social cognition, 37
social comparison, vii, 3, 21, 22, 23, 53, 54,
    60, 62, 63, 71
social comparison theory, vii, 3, 21, 22, 23,
    53, 54, 60
social consequences, 38
social development, 18
social environment, 8
social exchange, 5
social group, 72
social identity, vii, 3, 25, 41, 53, 70, 72
social identity theory, vii, 3, 53, 72
social influence, vii, 2, 9, 12, 18, 21, 22, 23,
    31, 41, 43, 53, 54, 58, 62, 70
social influences, 62, 70
social learning, vii, 3, 5, 7, 8, 9, 11, 53
social learning theory, vii, 3, 5, 53
social network, 23, 45, 47
social norms, 15, 22, 27, 28, 41, 50, 54, 60,
    61, 68, 69
social psychology, 65, 73
social structure, 45
socialization, 8, 29, 45, 46, 54, 69
spatial, 1
specificity, 26, 66, 72
statistics, 17
stigmatization, 29
stimulus, 5
strategies, 9, 13, 17, 18, 27, 43, 46, 52, 65,
    66, 67
stress, 46
structural equation model, 17
students, 1, 2, 6, 8, 9, 13, 17, 18, 22, 26, 27,
    28, 30, 34, 39, 42, 46, 47, 50, 51, 58, 60,
    63, 64, 65, 66, 67, 68, 69, 70, 71, 72, 73
subjective, 33, 34, 35, 37
substance use, 22, 30, 31, 45, 46, 57, 58, 59,
    61, 69, 71
substances, 7, 17, 46
syndrome, 16, 18, 73

T

tactics, 52
targets, 18, 39
teens, 58
television, 7, 62
therapists, 52
threatening, 21, 22, 49
threats, 49
tobacco, 16, 65, 67
training, 9, 46
trajectory, 59
transgression, 15, 17
transition, 70, 73
trial, 61, 66
typology, 38

U

unconventionality, 15
undergraduate, 34
university students, 27
upward comparisons, 22

V

valence, 13
validity, 35, 47, 70
values, 29, 41, 45
variables, 15, 17, 22, 34, 71
variance, 12, 13, 17, 18, 34, 35
variation, 58, 72
vulnerability, 45, 59

W

well-being, 60
women, 28

Y

young adults, vii, 1, 2, 3, 5, 6, 7, 8, 9, 12,
    18, 19, 22, 26, 28, 34, 35, 37, 38, 39, 43,
    49, 50, 51, 53, 54, 59, 61, 63, 65, 68